Bangladeshis in M...

Mustak Ahmed Mustafa

British Bangladeshi

Written & Compiled by Mustak Ahmed Mustafa
Copyright © Mustak Ahmed Mustafa 2021

Date of Publications
First published on 26 March 2013
Second published in November 2021
Published by: British Bangladeshi imprint of MAPublisher (Penzance), and will be entered into the British Bangladeshi Information Group (BBIG) catalogue.

ISBN-13: 978-1-910499-75-7

All rights reserved. No part of this publication may be reproduced, stored in a retrieval system, or transmitted, in any form or by any means, electronic, mechanical, photocopying, recording, public performances or otherwise, without prior written permission of the copyright holder, except for brief quotations embodied in critical articles or reviews.

Cover design supplied by Author, Mustak Ahmed Mustafa
Typeset in Times Roman

Paper printed on is FSC Certified, lead free, acid free, buffered paper made from wood based pulp. Our paper meets the ISO 9706 standard for permanent paper. As such, paper will last several hundred years when stored.

Dedication

This book is dedicated to those who are the inspiration for my writings, more specifically, to my parents. Also, dedication goes to those who I loved including family, friends, community activist, writers, and politicians.

Acknowledgements:

1. Melonie Tebbott – Manchester Metropolitan University.
2. Dr. Robert Light – Huddersfield University
3. Jalal Uddin – ITC – Xtreme PC
4. Shofique Miah, Nazia Kadiri, Nor Tasneem Abdul Wahab – Blue3print
5. Ahad Ullah Shah – City Brokers UK
6. Iqbal Ahmed – Sonali Bank UK Ltd
7. Yousuf Miah – Event Management
8. Khukon Maskub – Supreme & Co
9. Andrew Schofield - North West Sound Archive
10. Jamal Uddin – Westwood Restaurant
11. Murad Chowdhury – Photography.
12. Jamal Uddin – Degnasoft
13. Shahel Chowdhury – Infinite Marketing
14. Abdul Hamid – PBL Exchange UK Limited
15. Hasan Ahmed Chowdhury – Sylhet Travel Services
16. Juned Ahmed – Probash Bangla & Spice City
17. Phil Carey – Rathbone
18. Shahid Zaman – Regulus Training & Employment.
19. Abdul Mannan - Oly Oli Ltd
20. Muzahid Khan – Sylhet Times
21. Shahid Miah – Jonosheba Group
22. Nep Islam Shaek – British Asian Media Group
23. Koyes Shikder – Bangla Transcription Services
24. Fahima Sultana – Admin & Event Management
25. Abul Hasnath Shamin – Awards & Presentation
26. Hamidul Kibria Chowdhury – Publication
27. Suhel Khan – Black Rose Hotel, Uttara, Dhaka.

BUCKINGHAM PALACE

Dear Mr. Mustafa

The Queen has asked me to thank you for your letter of 8th February, telling Her Majesty about the forthcoming publication of the book Oral History of Bangladeshis in Greater Manchester, following the launch of the video version of this Heritage Lottery Funded project.

The culmination of this five-year project is no doubt a source of great pride for the Bangladeshi community in Greater Manchester, and I am to convey the Queen's congratulations and good wishes to you and everyone involved in this social and historical venture.

Please accept my warm good wishes for every success with the launch of the book.

Yours sincerely,

Mrs. Sonia Bonici
Senior Correspondence Officer

10 DOWNING STREET
LONDON SW1A 2AA
www.number10.gov.uk

26th March 2012

Dear Mr. Mustafa,

Thank you for your letter of 8th February 2012 to the Prime Minister about the "Oral History of Bangladeshis in Greater Manchester". I know that you are involved in undertaking a significant task in capturing the experiences of those who have come to this country and settled in Greater Manchester, often with very little, and how they have sought to make this country their home.

The Prime Minister is proud of the contribution that the British Bangladeshi community has made to this country's economic and social well-being. We need to draw on the skills and expertise of all people, whatever their background, as we respond to the current social and economic challenges Britain faces.

The Prime Minister is pleased that the Communities Minister, Andrew Stunell MP, has provided you with a supportive statement about this local project, and wishes you and your project every success for the future.

Yours sincerely

SIMON KING

PS for the Prime Minister David Cameron

Communities
and Local Government

Andrew Stunell MP
Parliamentary Under Secretary of State

Department for Communities and Local Government
Eland House
Bressenden Place
London SW1E 5DU

There is little doubt that Britain today is a far more diverse and tolerant society than it was a generation ago. The many and various communities that makeup Britain today energise our businesses and immeasurably enrich our cultural and social life. Your Bangladeshi Community is indeed a long-standing and welcome presence in our society and makes an important contribution to its continued prosperity.

The Government wants Britain to become a more integrated society, where we celebrate the things, we have in common. These include a society where everyone can achieve their aspirations and realise their potential, irrespective of their background, where everyone plays their part in social, civic, and economic life together, and where behaviours that run counter to our shared values can be challenged.

The Big Society will put more power and opportunities in people's hands. We need to draw on the skills and expertise of all people across the country as we respond to the social, political, and economic challenges Britain faces. As a government, we strongly encourage the different local partners to work together to drive action and to learn from each other in promoting integration and making a real difference in the lives of their communities.

Message from the John Penrose MP

Dear Mr. Mustafa,

The history and heritage of this country come in many forms. Our Castles and cathedrals and our literature and music all play a part and all come together as the legacy we pass on to our children and future generations. And the oral history of our diverse communities has a really important place in this tradition as well. So I am delighted to hear that the Tigers International Association has carried out the Oral History of Bangladeshis in Greater Manchester.

This Oral History Project explores and seeks to understand the integration of the Bangladeshi community within Manchester and beyond so that future generations can learn and reflect upon this and use it to prosper in a positive way within the community.

Yours sincerely

John Penrose MP
Minister for Tourism and Heritage

**ASSISTANT HIGH COMMISSION FOR THE
PEOPLE'S REPUBLIC OF BANGLADESH**

CEDAR HOUSE, 3RD FLOOR
2, FAIRFIELD STREET
MANCHESTER, M1 3GF
UNITED KINGDOM

Telephone No. 0161-236 4853

Message from the Assistant High Commissioner of Bangladesh to Manchester.

It gives me immense pleasure to know that initiative has already been taken by my countrymen with the help of different British organizations in collecting and afterward composing the "Oral History of Bangladeshis' in Greater Manchester". I do salute such an initiative.

As the proverb goes "It is better late than never", even the initiative is taken after around sixty years of available information of first migrants from Bangladesh to this part of the United Kingdom, the collection of information about the struggles and sacrifices of our ancestors will undoubtedly help us as well as our next generation to try to move towards then integration into this society and enlighten the image of Bangladesh as a whole.

We all learn from history and try to make our lives comfortable from the lessons learned. In this regard, I would like to take this opportunity to express my heartfelt gratitude to those who took the pain of providing their invaluable experience, time for interviews, and last but not least allowing their next generations to use and capitalize on their extremely hard-earned foundation on which the next generations could further advance their lives. I also would like to pay tribute and pray to the Almighty for the departed souls of those who also created the path of settlement for my countrymen, may the Almighty bestow peace on their departed souls.

Finally, I would like to express my heartfelt felicitations to the Chairperson and Programme Manager and his able colleagues for their relentless hard work for bringing such an extraordinary effort into reality by bringing the publication of "Oral History of Bangladeshis' in Greater Manchester". I also thank all concerned for their commendable efforts in this historic endeavour.

(Zokey Ahad)
Assistant High Commissioner

EUROPEAN PARLIAMENT

The Great in Greater Manchester comes from the diversity of our communities and it is important that we celebrate this. There are long and binding links between Bangladesh and Greater Manchester which grow and strengthen each year.

As a Member of the European Parliament, I have many friends in the Bangladeshi community, councillors I work with here and across the North West. I want to take this opportunity to thank you for everything you do to contribute to the economic and political life of our region as councillors, doctors, lawyers, community groups, voluntary organisations, teachers, and mayors!

Tigers International Association must be congratulated for their documenting of the oral history of Bangladeshis in Greater Manchester. We know, unlike those preaching prejudice, hate, and division, that our diversity is our strength, and it is important that we acknowledge the contribution of all communities to the past, current, and future success of our region.

This Oral History celebrates the role and many achievements of the Bangladeshi community recognising the progress that has been made. It also sets an example for future generations of Bangladeshis in Greater Manchester, allowing them to learn from and reflect on the experiences of their parents, grandparents, and great-grandparents.

However, this book is not only an important history for the Bangladeshi Community it is a fantastic tool for teaching and learning in the wider community about the positive impact and role our diverse communities have in our region.
Thank you for you all you have done to make our region a great place.

Arlene McCarthy MEP

"For centuries, the world over, long before the written word was common place, storytellers have passed down the history of their culture and community.

From the Inuit in the frozen North to the Aborigines in Australasian deserts, people have gathered around their home fires, children listening spellbound, to the tales of their forebears that they, in turn, would pass down the generations.

But the world has changed. Accessible long-distance travel has made it easy to migrate across the globe. Film, television, computers, and the internet have changed communications forever.

Whenever people uproot themselves, travelling to build new homes and new lives on the other side of the world, they take with them their traditions, culture, and history, keeping these alive whilst embracing their new community's lifestyle.

We have a long-established Bangladeshi community in Greater Manchester. Since 1950's the mill towns of the North have become home to immigrants from many countries, particularly South Asia. These new generations are part of Britain's rich diversity, but it is still just as important for those who moved here in search of jobs and a better life, to pass on just how and why they came to uproot themselves and what they found when they arrived. In recording the oral history of these settlers, The Tigers International Association - TIA is keeping alive this great tradition of storytelling.

Each new generation faces its challenges and today oral history can be recorded on digital media. It brings educational benefits, embracing personal history, political commentary, and evolving culture.

I thank all from The Tigers International Association and those who told their stories, to bring together this extensive, demanding exercise, taking a great tradition and transforming it to be just as relevant in the 21st century."

Sajjad Karim MEP LLB (Hons)
Conservative Member of the European Parliament - North West of England

Debbie Abrahams

HOUSE OF COMMONS

I am extremely pleased to welcome this study as it is an important step in understanding the experiences of those who migrated to Greater Manchester from Bangladesh during the 1950s and beyond. I also hope it will be of interest to all those who wish to understand how Britain developed as a multi-cultural society throughout the second half of the 20th century. I have no doubt this will prove to be an invaluable educational resource.

This project, charting the experiences of first-generation migrants from Bangladesh, leaves a valuable legacy for future generations in helping to understand the origins of an important and valuable group within our diverse national and local community. I hope that with greater understanding can come greater tolerance and positive integration between communities, continuing the progress already made.

The Bangladeshi community has always made valuable contributions to the life and culture of the United Kingdom, and I do not doubt that they will continue to do so for many years to come. In the face of sceptics of multiculturalism and the worrying rise of the far-right in some areas of Europe, we must be forthright in acknowledging the valuable contribution which is made by all the cultures which make up our national identity.

As I am sure this book will testify, those who first arrived in Britain over 50 years ago faced a great range of challenges. The challenges faced by the Bangladeshi community today are quite different. Yet the strength of the community, illustrated by groups such as the Tigers International Association and the broad coalition who have supported this project, will come together to help to meet those challenges. Together we can continue our co-operation into the 21st century to build a stronger community in Greater Manchester. It gives me great pleasure to be able to work with you in achieving this worthwhile goal.

Debbie Abrahams MP
Oldham East and Saddleworth

The Rt Hon Michael Meacher MP

HOUSE OF COMMONS

Oldham over the years has changed a great deal. I think that many people travelling here from Bangladesh many years ago would have found a place filled with smoking mill chimneys and the sounds of factory sirens calling people to work. Indeed, many people from Bangladesh travelling to Oldham then would no doubt have found work in those very same mills and factories, just as others were responsible for introducing Bangladeshi cuisine to the locals by opening some of our best restaurants; a tradition that still exists today in the very thriving area of Westwood.

I know that the Bangladeshi community now goes out into the wider world to earn their living and take great pride in the educational and other facilities open to them. However, without the people who came before to help and guide them, their lives would not be as rich and we, therefore, should always be grateful to those that paved the way.

Oldham is a very diverse town with people from many different cultures living side by side and all the different communities have had an impact on how the town has developed through the years. It is therefore of great interest to hear the stories of those who first came here and to hear their views on how things have changed and what their concerns are today.

I think the Oral History project will prove to be a very useful piece of information not only for people today, and not only for the Bangladeshi Community but for future generations of the town.

The TIA is to be congratulated for all the work they have done, as should all the people who have participated in the project. Well done to everyone involved.

Yours sincerely

Michael Meacher

The Rt Hon Michael Meacher MP
Oldham West & Royton

S Danczuk MP

HOUSE OF COMMONS

Dear Mustak

I am delighted to hear that the Tigers International Association has carried out the Oral History of Bangladeshis in Greater Manchester. "The Oral History Project is unique and diverse as it explores and understands the integration of the Bangladeshi community within Manchester so future generations can reflect upon this and continue to prosper in a positive way within the community.

The project sets a perfect example for future generations to acknowledge and follow. As a whole Greater Manchester has benefitted, and this is due to TIA, Manchester Metropolitan University, and other partnerships linked to the project and the members of the community who allowed their story to be documented.

S. Danczuk
Rochdale's Member of Parliament"

Jonathan Reynolds MP

HOUSE OF COMMONS

"This is an exciting project that will provide a lasting record of the experiences of the Bangladeshi community in Greater Manchester.

"For those outside the Bangladeshi community, this 'Oral History of Bangladeshis in Greater Manchester provides a rare and unique insight into what it is like to settle in a new country.

"But it will also play a vital part in enabling these experiences to be passed on from generation to generation for many years to come.

"Of course many younger members of the Bangladeshi community can still hear firsthand accounts of what it was like to settle in the UK directly from their elders.

"But this will not always be the case – and this valuable piece of research will help to ensure these precious and unique experiences should not be forgotten.

"I believe the 'Oral History of Bangladeshis in Greater Manchester will be of wide interest to those living in Greater Manchester, whether they are a part of the Bangladeshi community or not.

"I congratulate the Tigers International Association on their work – and I look forward to reading it."

Jonathan Reynolds MP
Member of Parliament for Stalybridge and Hyde

John Leech MP

HOUSE OF COMMONS

Oral History of the Bangladeshis in Greater Manchester

I am proud to be an MP in such a diverse, multi-cultural city like Manchester, and I am proud to represent a vibrant Bangladeshi community. Manchester's first councillor of Bangladeshi descent was my Liberal Democrat colleague Abu Choudhury, who served as a Rusholme councillor and was awarded an MBE by the Queen for his services to the Bangladeshi community here in Manchester.

In my seven years as an MP, I have worked with the Bangladeshi community on many issues – whether it be supporting the work of the community in Manchester or helping raise money for health and education projects in Bangladesh. In August and September 2010, I also had the chance to visit Bangladesh with Voluntary Services Overseas.

I spent 10 days in Khulna and Dhaka supporting projects aimed at improving women's workers' rights in the vastly expanding shrimp industry and the impact of this expansion of the industry on flooding in the region. The expansion of shrimp production has resulted in the banks of many of Bangladesh's watercourses being weakened as more and more shrimp pools are created. This has a potentially devastating impact when the floods come, as the riverbanks cannot withstand the force of the water, having been weakened by more and more makeshift channels to the new shrimp ponds.

My main memories of Bangladesh were the incessant humidity, the constant hum of noise in the city, and the indefatigable spirit of the people. You cannot begin to imagine what the country is like without having the opportunity to enjoy it first-hand.

This book is a great opportunity for the Bangladeshi Community to share its collective experiences with future generations. It builds on the huge contribution they have made to Manchester's life, and I am happy to support it.

Tony Lloyd MP

HOUSE OF COMMONS

Dear Mustak

Greater Manchester can rightly claim to have been built by migrants. People have come from the most diverse backgrounds, some fleeing tyranny, many fleeing poverties, or simply hoping for a better life. And each individual and each community has played its role and left its mark on what modern Manchester and its surroundings are all about.

The Bangladeshi community of Greater Manchester has a unique history, and this is made up of the struggles of real people. In telling their stories, the authors have made sure that they are remembered for what they are, experiences of real people. It is important to recognise that it would not have been possible without willing participants eager to share their personal stories to contribute to the history of a community. Oral history depends on the willingness of people to share the personal and the book pays fitting testimony to the personal struggles of the individuals involved.

In the early years, people left what was East Bengal in British India to join the British Army or Merchant Navy and untold numbers gave their lives in the First and Second World Wars. Later men came from East Pakistan arriving on their own and working hard in the textile mills and restaurants sending money home to their families, and planning to return home. That generation experienced loneliness and racism that was too widespread low pay, and poverty. But there was a joy as well. Joy, when family reunions saw the slow trickle of wives and families, become a steady stream. Joy as children built on the sacrifices of their parents and began to achieve in business, in politics, and the professions. I well recall the cries of "Joy Bangla" when British Bangladeshis celebrated the birth of the new nation of Bangladesh.

These years on, when I look at the young and the not so young who rightly and proudly are British Bangladeshis, those early years and early struggles seem far distant.

The very first generation of Bangladeshis who came to Manchester would find today's Manchester very different from their own. It is certainly the case that the UK and Greater Manchester, in particular, is much more inclusive and diverse but we should not downplay the reality that there are still disadvantages to overcome and struggles to fight and win but Manchester's Bangladeshi community is a permanent reality and is well equipped to face today's challenges precisely because everyone owes a debt to the early pioneers who laid those early foundations.

In creating a link between our previous and future generations, this book is a real service not only to the Bangladeshi community but to all who love Greater Manchester.

Rt Hon Hazel Blears MP

HOUSE OF COMMONS

Message from Hazel Blears

Dear Mustak

"I welcome this important project and believe it will help to highlight the valuable contribution that the Bangladeshi community has made to Greater Manchester."

Best wishes

Rt Hon Hazel Blears MP
Salford

Message from Manchester Metropolitan University

Manchester Metropolitan University

I am writing to express support for your proposed funding application to develop an oral and community history project with the Bangladeshi community in Greater Manchester. This is welcome and exciting news, which promises to make an important contribution to understanding the community's origins and settlement in the region.

Staff in the Manchester Centre for Regional History have many years' experience of working with groups in the city to develop local history projects of various sorts and we found the recent meeting to discuss your proposal extremely encouraging. We feel there and urgent need for well-planned community-based projects of this sort which give historical profile of the community itself.

Your project promises to make a particular contribution to Manchester's rich heritage of migration and settlement, significantly adding to the stories of the many communities which have contributed to the making of the city. We hope it will be successful and are very happy to give our backing to your application.

Best wishes

Melanie Tebbutt

Director
The Manchester Centre for Regional History

University of HUDDERSFIELD

The message of Support for 'An Oral history of Bangladeshis in Greater Manchester' Of the many important initiatives to be undertaken by the Tiger's international Association, the HLF funded 'Oral history of Bangladeshis in Greater Manchester' project is amongst the most significant. As the acclaimed oral historian, Alistair Thompson has written a 'central and abiding claim of oral historians of migration has been that the migrant's own story is likely to be unrecorded or ill-documented, and that oral evidence provides an essential record of the hidden history of migration.' The 'Oral history of Bangladeshis in Greater Manchester' project has enabled the men and women who came to North West England from Bangladesh to tell their own story in a unique collection of oral testimonies which provide the focal point of this fascinating book.

The interviews offer an absorbing account of how and why people left Bangladesh during the second half of the twentieth century and the difficult circumstances they often encountered upon arriving in their new home. Most came from rural backgrounds and found themselves living in urban industrialized areas of Greater Manchester where they took what work they could, often in local factories. Many also faced financial hardship as well as language and cultural barriers. But one common theme throughout the interviews is the determination of those who shared their memories to overcome these difficulties in order to build a new life for themselves and provide better opportunities for their families and other members of their community. The interviews describe how through individual and collective efforts they established businesses, places of worship, and other community institutions which have enabled members of their own and subsequent generations to make significant contributions to the Bangladeshi community and British society in general.

Through this book and the collection of oral history interviews on which it is based an essential record of one of the key communities which make up multicultural Britain in the 21st century has been preserved. Each represents an irreplaceable resource not only for future generations of the Bangladeshi community with an interest in their heritage but also for anyone looking to develop a wider understanding of British Social History.

Dr. Robert Light
Centre for Visual and Oral History Research
University of Huddersfield

Bangladesh Parliament,
Parliament House
Shere-e-Bangla Nagar
Dhaka 1207, Bangladesh

Message from the Honourable Deputy Speaker Shawkat Ali MP

I am delighted to learn that Mr. Mustak Ahmed Mustafa is publishing a book called "History of Bangladeshis in Greater Manchester". I have gone through the manuscript of the book and I found that this is an impressive book through which the lifestyle of the first-generation Bangladeshi's living in the UK, their struggle and happiness have brilliantly portrayed. This book presents an account of memories of the first-generation Bangladeshi's living in the Greater Manchester area of the UK.

This project brought together a unique set of first-generation Bangladeshis' who settled in the Greater Manchester area, who gave a snapshot of the types of life and experiences. I would like to offer my heartfelt thanks to them and their families for supporting this project and helping the TIA to record their journey for generations to come.

I believe that the experience of the first generation of Bangladeshis will be a good resource for the researchers or even the Bangladeshi generations to come to understand their roots and how they are living in Britain. The author has gathered very important information about our history which we can proudly and celebrated by the present and future generations to come.

I would like to thank all the participants, volunteers, and workers of Tigers International Association – TIA, for undertaking a unique piece of work, which will be preserved and reached to all communities in the UK and abroad. I hope the devoted efforts of the author will be awarded success.

Ministry of Education
Government of Bangladesh

MESSAGE FROM THE RT. HONOURABLE EDUCATION MINISTER NURUL ISLAM NAHID MP

I am delighted to learn that Mustak Ahmed Mustafa is publishing a book with the title of History of Bangladeshis in Greater Manchester. I have gone through the manuscript of the book, and I found that this is an impressive book through which the lifestyle of the first-generation Bangladeshi expatriates in the UK, their socio-cultural, economic conditions, and their agony and happiness have vibrantly portrayed.

The author has earned name and fame as a prolific writer. This publication will particularly be helpful to our new generation, which is not aware of the history, culture, and tradition of Bangladesh & the settlement history of Bangladeshis in the United Kingdom.

I would like to take the opportunity to thank all the participants, volunteers, and workers of Tigers International Association – TIA, for undertaking an exclusive piece of work, which will be preserved and reached to all communities in the UK and across the world.

The author has gathered very important information about the history of first-generation Bangladeshis settled in the UK and making huge contributions to society, which we can proudly and celebrated by the present and future generations to come. This book is a great opportunity for the researchers, colleges, universities to share their collective experiences for their studies.

I also would like to give special thanks to the writer for his valuable contribution and hope the enthusiastic efforts of the author will be awarded accomplishment with gratitude.

Ministry of Expatriate's welfare and overseas employment
71-72, Old Elephant Road, Eskaton Garden, Dhaka
Message from Engineer Khandaker Musharaf Hussain MP

I am delighted to learn that Mr. Mustak Ahmed Mustafa is publishing a book called "First Generation of Bangladeshis in Greater Manchester". I have gone through the manuscript of the book, and I found this is an extraordinary book through which the lifestyle of the first-generation Bangladeshi expatriates in the UK, their socio-cultural, economic conditions, and their agony and happiness have vibrantly portrayed.

The writer has captured the conversations in audio and video and they have been archived and captured in DVD format so that they are preserved for years to come. They have already proven to be an excellent tool for our youngsters to learn about their past and an educational tool for everyone in Manchester and around the world, who is interested in tracing the rich diversity of the people in the UK.

I am aware that the Tigers International Association – TIA has worked tirelessly on this project. Their commitment was a fitting testimony to those they were researching, interviewing, and working with. I believe they will work with schools, libraries, and other organisations to get this resource to large audiences so that these experiences can be shared and appreciated. TIA has hoped that similar projects will spring up elsewhere so that the rich history of Bangladeshis in Britain can be truly captured, shared, and celebrated.

The author has earned name and fame as a creative writer. The publication of this history book will particularly be helpful to our new generation, which is not aware of the history, culture, and tradition of Bangladesh and Britain. It also provides important information about how the Bangladeshis started migrating to the UK and got settled there to earn a livelihood. The author has gathered our history which we can proudly and celebrated by the present and future generations to come.

I thank all participants, volunteers, and workers of Tigers International Association – TIA, for undertaking a unique piece of work, which will be preserved and reached to all communities in the UK and across the world. I hope the dedicated efforts of the author will be crowned with success.

Ministry of Foreign Affairs
Government of Bangladesh

MESSAGE FROM THE RT. HONOURABLE FOREIGN MINISTER DR. DIPU MONI MP

I am pleased to learn that Mustak Ahmed Mustafa is publishing a book "History of Bangladeshis in Greater Manchester". I found that this is a remarkable book through which the life experience of the first-generation Bangladeshi expatriates in the UK has been presented very well.

The author has gathered very important information about the history of first-generation Bangladeshis settled in the UK. I am sure, that this publication will be useful to our researchers, colleges, universities, government, and voluntary organisation to share its valuable information. It will also be reached to all communities in the UK and across the world.

The Tigers International Association – TIA, has done tremendous achievements by undertaking this research project, which we can proudly and celebrated by the present and future generations to come. I am very much hoping that they will continue to do their good work.

Finally, I would like to thank the writer for his valuable contribution, and the passionate efforts of the author will be honoured with appreciation.

Bangladesh Nationalist Party – BNP
28 VIP Road, Naya Paltan
Dhaka-1000, Bangladesh

Message from Mirza Fokhrul Islam Alamgir – Acting General Secretary – Bangladesh Nationalist Party

I am tremendously pleased to welcome this publication of "History of Bangladeshis in Greater Manchester", which is a research project undertaken by the Tigers International Association – TIA. I have no doubt this will be a very useful educational resource for the wider community.

This book highlights the experiences of first-generation migrants from Bangladesh, leaves a valuable legacy for future generations to share the information and help themselves to improve their lives and make a positive contribution to society. The Bangladeshi community has always made valuable contributions to the life and culture of the United Kingdom and I do not doubt that they will continue to do so for many years to come.

As I am sure this book will bear witness, those who the first generation settled in Great Britain and faced a great range of challenges by the Bangladeshi community. The author has gathered significant information about the history of first-generation Bangladeshis settled in the UK and making enormous contributions to the society, which we can proudly and celebrated by the present and future generations to come. This book is a great opportunity for the researchers, colleges, universities to share their collective experiences for their studies.

I am delighted to learn that Mustak Ahmed Mustafa made his valuable contribution by publishing this book. I would like to give special thanks to the writer for his passionate efforts, which will be appreciated and recognised by the wider community with gratitude.

University of Dhaka
Nilkhet Rd, Dhaka,
Bangladesh

Message from the professor AAMS Arefin Siddique

I am delighted to learn that Mustak Ahmed Mustafa is publishing a book "History of Bangladeshis in Greater Manchester". I have gone through the manuscript of the history book and I found this is an inspiring book through which the lifestyle of the first-generation Bangladeshi's living in the UK, their socio-cultural, economic conditions, and their agony and happiness have vibrantly portrayed.

As I am aware the author has earned name and fame as a prolific writer. The History of Bangladeshis in Greater Manchester is a tremendously significant project that charted the settlement of Bangladeshis in this area of the UK. This project has enabled them to be captured invaluable experiences of people who paved the way for generations with their experiences in a foreign land. It has enabled them to recognize the pioneering early migrants to the UK. By writing this history book they have acknowledged the participants' achievements and shown gratitude to them for creating the future the public enjoys today.

This publication will particularly be helpful for the researchers, academics and all other government and non-government institutions to use this book as a reference to do further study in this area. It is also providing significant information about how the Bangladeshi's settled in the UK and earn the livelihood. The author has gathered the history which we can proudly and celebrated by the present and future generations to come.

I would like to thank all the Bangladeshi participants, volunteers, and workers of Tigers International Association – TIA, for undertaking a distinctive piece of work, which will be reached to all communities across the world. I also would like to give special thanks to the writer for his valuable contribution and hope the dedicated hard work of the author will be recognised by the institution with success.

University of Dhaka
Nilkhet Rd, Dhaka,
Bangladesh

Message from Professor Dr. Md. Anwarul Islam

Dear Mr. Mustafa
I came to learn that the book Oral History of Bangladeshis in Greater Manchester is a unique research book in recent years. This publication in the form of a book provides a lot of information about the Bangladeshis who are living in Greater Manchester.

No doubt this book is a source of great pride for the Bangladeshis. We the Bangladeshis feel very proud of it.

Through this book, each learned people who will read this will be able to know the British Bangladeshi Community and their economic and social well-being.

Many thanks to Mustafa for his skills and expertise endeavours''. I hope that this type of further study will extend the knowledge not only in Greater Manchester but also the whole U.K. in the future.
Yours Sincerely

Prof. Dr. Md. Anwarul Islam

MESSAGE FROM THE SYLHET CITY MAYOR ARIFUL HAQUE CHOWDHURY

I am delighted to learn that Mustak Ahmed Mustafa is publishing a book with the title of History of Bangladeshis in Greater Manchester. I have gone through the manuscript of the book, and I found this is an impressive book through which the lifestyle of the first-generation Bangladeshi expatriates in the UK, their socio-cultural, economic conditions, and their agony and happiness have vibrantly portrayed. This book presents an account of memories of the cross-section of Bangladeshi expatriates living in Greater Manchester.

The author of many books and has earned name and fame as a prolific writer. The publication of this history book will particularly be helpful to our new generation, which is not aware of the history, culture, and tradition of Bangladesh and Great Britain. It is also providing important information about how the Bangladeshis started migrating to the UK and got settled there to earn a livelihood. The author has gathered very important information about our history which we can proudly and celebrated by the present and future generations to come.

I would like to thank all the participants, volunteers, and workers of Tigers International Association – TIA, for undertaking a unique piece of work, which will be preserved and reached to all communities in the UK and across the world. I also would like to give special thanks to the writer for his valuable contribution and hope the dedicated efforts of the author will be crowned with success.

Contents

Dedication	3
Acknowledgements:	4
Preface	33
Summary Of History Project	35
Chapter I – Introduction	37
1.1　Introduction About The Organisation:	37
1.2 Introduction Of The Oral History Project:	40
1.3　Objectives:	41
1.4　Introduction Of The Author:	42
Chapter 2 – Research And Analysis:	45
2.1　Analytical Framework:	45
2.2　Melting Pot, Cultural Mosaic, And Multiculturalism:	45
2.3　Diaspora And Trans-Nationalism:	46
2.4　Source Of Information:	46
2.4.1　Individual Participants:	47
2.4.2　Government:	47
2.4.3　Academic/Community Based Organisations:	47
2.5　Research Methodology:	48
2.5.1　Gathering Of Primary Data:	48
2.5.2　Gathering Of Secondary Information:	50
2.5.3　Organisation Of The Publication Of History Book:	50
Chapter 3: History & Culture	51
3.1 History Of Bangladesh:	51
3.2　Architecture:	52
3.3　Literature:	52
3.4　Art:	53
3.5　Music:	54
3.6　Dance:	55
3.7　Drama:	55
3.8.　Religion:	56
3.8.1　Islam:	56
3.8.2　Hinduism:	57
3.8.3　Buddhism:	57
3.8.4　Christianity:	58
3.9　Customs And Traditions Of Bangladesh:	58
3.9.1　Naming Ceremony:	59
3.9.2　Nabanna (New Rice):	59
3.9.3　Pahela Baishakh (Bengali New Year):	59
3.10.　Religious Customs:	60
3.10.1　Akika (Islamic):	60
3.10.2　Mussalmani Or Khatna (Circumcision):	60

3.10.3 After Death:	60
3.11. Religious Celebrations:	60
3.11.1 Shob-E-Barat:	60
3.11.2 Ramadan:	61
3.11.3 Shob-E-Qadar:	61
3.11.4 Eid-Ul-Fitr:	61
3.11.5 Hajj (Pilgrimage To Makkah):	62
3.11.6 Eid-Ul-Azha:	62
3.11.7 Eid-E-Miladunnabi:	63
3.11.8 Durga Puja:	63
3.11.9 Christmas:	63
3.12 Shaheed Day (Language Day):	64
3.13 Independence & National Day:	65
3.14 The Victory Day:	66
3.15 Conclusion:	66
Chapter 4 - Bangladeshis In English Law	67
4.1 Abstract:	67
4.2 The Interplay Of Legal Systems Or Bangladeshi Legal Pluralism:	67
4.2.1 Immigration Restrictions	70
4.3 Bangladeshis In English Law	74
4.3.1 Sanctity Of Marriage Or Over-Reliance On Kagzi Evidence?	75
4.3.2 Questioning The Legitimacy Of Children:	76
Glossary Of Terms:	80
Chapter 5 – Migration In The Uk	81
5.1 Bangladeshi Immigrants:	81
5.2 Global Bangladeshi Immigration:	81
5.2.1 Number:	81
5.2.2 Number Of Bangladeshi Immigrants	82
5.3 Bangladeshi Immigrants In The Uk:	82
5.3.1 History Of Immigration:	83
5.3.2 Pioneer Migrants Of Bangladeshis:	83
5.3.3 Number Of Bangladeshi Immigrants In The Uk:	84
5.3.4 Estimate Of Growth Of Bangladeshi Population	85
5.4. Geographical Coverage:	85
5.4.1 Socio-Economic Profile:	85
5.4.2 Labour Force Participation And Unemployment:	87
5.4.3 Remittance Flow:	88
5.4.4 Year-Wise Growth Of Remittance Flow	88
5.4.5 Year-Wise Remittance Flow Of Wage Earners	88
5.5 Conclusion	88
Chapter 6 - British Bangladeshi	90
6.1 History Of Bangladeshis In The United Kingdom:	91
6.2 Population:	94

6.4 Employment And Education: 96
6.5 Health And Housing: 96
6.6 Origins: 97
6.7 Culture: 98
6.8 Celebrations: 98
   6.8.1 The Language Movement Day (Shaheed Dibosh): 99
6.9 Marriage 100
6.10 Media 101
6.11 Religion: 101
6.12 Festivals: 102
6.13 Bangladeshi Society: 103
   6.13.1 Contribution: 103
   6.13.2 Political Identity 109
6.14 Business: 111
6.15 Curry Industry: 111
6.16　Bangladeshi Cuisine: 113
6.17　Regional Cuisines: 114
6.18　Staple Ingredients And Spices: 115
6.19　Other Famous Bangladeshi Dishes 116
6.20　Sweets And Desserts: 116
6.21　Beverages 117
6.22　Local Businesses: 117
6.23　Media: 118
6.24　Remittance: 118
6.25 Conclusion: 119
Chapter 7 - Greater Manchester Communities 120
7.1- Greater Manchester: 122
   7.1.1 - History 123
   7.1.2 - Industrial Revolution 128
   7.1.3 - Growth Of The Textile Trade 130
   7.1.4 - Population 133
   7.1.5 - Demography 133
   7.1.6 - Culture 135
   7.1.7 - Economy 136
   7.1.7 - Social History 136
   7.1.8 - Education 138
   7.1.9 - Economy 139
   7.1.10 - Map 140
7.2 - Oldham 140
   7.2.1 – History 141
   7.2.2 - Industrial Revolution 142
   7.2.3 - Growth Of Textile Trade 144
   7.2.4 - Population 146

7.2.5 – Demography	147
7.2.6 - Culture	147
7.2.7 - Social History	149
7.2.8 - Education	151
7.2.9 - Economy	151
7.2.10 - Map	153
7.3 – Rochdale	153
7.3.1 - History	154
7.3.2 - Industrial Revolution	155
7.3.3 - Growth Of Textile Trade	156
7.3.4 - Population	156
7.3.5 - Demography	157
7.3.6 - Education	157
7.3.7 – Map	158
7.4 – Tameside:	158
7.4.1 – History:	159
7.4.2 - Industrial Revolution	160
7.4.3 - Population	160
7.4.4 - Demography	162
7.4.5 – Culture	162
7.4.6 - Social History	163
7.4.7 - Education	164
7.4.8 - Economy	165
7.4.9 - Map	167
7.5 - Salford	167
7.5.1 - History	168
7.5.2 - Industrial Revolution	170
7.5.3 - Growth Of Textile Trade	172
7.5.4 - Population	172
7.5.5 - Demography	173
7.5.6 - Culture	174
7.5.7 - Education	174
7.5.8 - Economy	175
7.5.9 - Map	177
7.6 – Conclusion	177
Bibliography	178
References	179
Source Of Information From Internet:	184
Mapublisher Catalogue	187

Preface

It gives me great pleasure to introduce you to one of the most important project Tigers International Association - TIA has undertaken in its 20-year history. This project will be an addition to the existing local history and all the community will be benefitted not only locally, but globally.

The Oral History of Bangladeshis in Greater Manchester is a hugely significant project that charted the arrival and settlement of Bangladeshis in this area of the UK. What this project has enabled us to do is capture the invaluable experiences of people who paved the way for generations with their experiences in a foreign land. It has enabled us to recognise the pioneering early migrants to the UK. By writing this history book we are acknowledging their achievements and thanking them for creating the future the public enjoys today.

Of course, this history project would not be possible without all those people who participated and gave us an insight into their lives. It would not have been possible if we were not successful with the help from the Heritage Lottery Fund and subsequently the support of many partners, volunteers, sponsors, and supporters. We extend a very heartfelt thank you to all the people who were involved in and had supported us with this project.

This project brought together a unique set of first-generation Bangladeshis' who settled in the Greater Manchester area. We could have done hundreds of interviews and gathered the experiences of many more but naturally there were limitations in resources. Those that did participate were a cross-section of the very diverse group of first-generation Bangladeshis' who give us a snapshot of the types of life and experiences.

We offer our heartfelt thanks to them and their families for supporting this project and helping to preserve their journey for generations to come. The success of this project is down to the many people, businesses, and organisations that have supported us from day one. Without the commitments, resources, and generosity of the sponsors, we would not be able to accomplish the project.

This "Oral History of Bangladeshis' in Greater Manchester" project has been in our thoughts for several years but without the resources and support, we would not have been able to realise the potential that we have unlocked.

We have acknowledged the support of the Heritage Lottery Fund (HLF) to undertake the unique history project. What the HLF has enabled us to do is capture a piece of history that will now remain with us for years and play a role in educating and informing others of the history and origins of the people that make up the diversity and richness of Greater Manchester. Now we can present to you the findings of our project.

Our objective is to record the previous history from the first generation of the Bangladeshi people for the benefit of the wider community to share the experience. Also, this will be a good resource for the researcher or even the Bangladeshi generations to come to understand their roots and how they are living in Britain.

Summary of History Project

Early settlers in Greater Manchester from the Indian subcontinent can trace their roots back to nearly 100 years. The first wave of migrants in sizeable numbers from Bangladesh came in the 50's. It is over 70 years since and many of those early migrants are no longer with us. As they have passed, so have their experiences, hardships, and successes.

15 years ago, a group of people at Tigers International Association considered a project which could capture and keep some of the experiences so that future generations could see how the experiences of the past, first generations helped to shape their lives.

As ever, funding and resources held the project back. However, 14 years ago, we received support from the Heritage Lottery Fund to help us undertake the Oral History of Bangladeshis in Greater Manchester. This would capture accounts of the lives and experiences of some of that first generation, early settlers into the area. The aim was to obtain this invaluable information and keep it alive and with it, the memories of so many who have helped to make this area what it is: a rich, vibrant, and dynamic place.

We put together a team of dedicated people, researchers to find people with an interesting tale to tell. We found many. Sadly, we could only work with a limited number. Over 4 years, we spoke to no less than 50 people about their life, early days, experiences, hardships, and much more. They gave us an insight that was eye-opening, fascinating, full of happiness, and sadness, hardship and hope, and aspiration.

To undertake this very demanding piece of work, we worked with a range of agencies that supported us in a variety of ways including The Manchester Metropolitan University& Huddersfield University, local colleges, businesses, and voluntary organisations.

We captured the conversations in audio and video, and they have been archived and captured in DVD format so that they are preserved for years to come. They have already proven to be an excellent tool for our youngsters to learn about their past and an educational tool for everyone in Manchester who is interested in tracing the rich diversity of the people of this area.

All this has been made possible by the volunteers who have worked tirelessly on this project. Their commitment was a fitting testimony to those they were researching, interviewing, and working with. We will work with schools, libraries, and other organisations to get this resource to large audiences so that these experiences can be shared and appreciated. It is hoped that similar projects will spring up elsewhere so that the rich history of Bangladeshis in Britain can be truly captured, shared, and celebrated.

CHAPTER 1 – INTRODUCTION

1.1 Introduction about the Organisation:

Tigers International Association – TIA was formed by a group of British Bangladeshi professionals, inspired to work with and help Bangladeshi people residing in the UK and abroad. We are working with local government offices and other various voluntary organisations to provide support in the field of education, employment, health, leisure, and recreation.

TIA is based at 259 Featherstall Road North, Oldham, a terraced property, which has been adapted to provide office space together with a moderately sized meeting room. Its Management Committee is drawn from members of the local community, and the services that it provides benefit the local community.

It is a registered charity that has been in existence for over 12 years. Since it was founded, TIA and its team of volunteers have worked tirelessly to support the Bangladeshi community in the Greater Manchester area with advice, guidance, and basic training to empower people to play their part in society.

Over the 10 years of its existence, the TIA has created and still enjoys many useful and strong partnerships which help it to deliver real benefits and services to the residents of the Greater Manchester community.

Our charity is simple, supportive, and effective. Our objective is to increase confidence in education and better chances in life. TIA is based in Oldham to primarily work with the local people and make a positive impact in the community

TIA's vision for the organisation was sixth-fold. Firstly, to promote the benefit of the public especially the Bengali community in the UK and abroad without distinction of sex, race, religion, political or other opinions by associating together with the public and voluntary organisations in a common effort to advance education, training, leisure, and recreation.

Secondly, to work with the Bangladeshi community in the UK and abroad to create a social network to share the cultures of the various host communities to propagate understanding and tolerance by educating people in the cultural diversity of various communities and promoting understanding of the different cultures of the world (community cohesion).

Thirdly, The relief of persons who are in need by the provision of advice and information in such matters as immigration, money debts, welfare benefits, housing, health, education, training, and employment.

Fourthly, TIA aims to provide relief, whenever necessary to the victims of natural disasters of any community in the world.

Fifthly, advance the education of the public in the arts and cultural activities in particular through exhibitions, workshops, and performances to promote the development of a public appreciation of music, drama, and literature.

Sixthly, TIA's aims are to advance education and provide relief of unemployment for the benefit of the public by the establishment of an institution to deliver vocational training courses, provide work experience, and develop relationships with job centres, employers, and other agencies to provide assistance to find employment.

More specifically, TIA working with the local community and setting up various educational training, and providing efficient help and support within Education, Training, and advice projects based on local needs or community would benefit from.

TIA is focusing on developing activities in each of the areas; advice centre, training, and community projects. We want to take advantage of our unique emphasis on educational and cultural learning and development opportunities.

This is truly being a community-based charity organisation with membership open to individuals who will share our aims and objectives. General members are recruited to the TIA development committee, which has been formed. Through these local committees, a professional network has already been created. This will help immensely in delivering TIA's objectives.

TIA strengths are ongoing support from volunteers, effective financial management, effective communications between staff and community members, the heart of the community, and only organisation aiming primarily for Bangladeshi people although open to all, strong link with Local authority and other committee members, well known and respected organisation activities, and proven track record over 10 years of community and voluntary activities.

Over the years, the TIA has gained the respect of local people who rely heavily on the services including advice and information. TIA successfully delivered numerous projects for the benefit of local people, working with the statutory and voluntary sectors and the business community. This partnership approach has enabled it to go further and faster in helping people meet a variety of needs.

TIA's aim is to promote volunteering and provide opportunities for individuals to become involved in volunteering activities. TIA's aim is to provide a great standard of customer service to its communities and provide them with a simple effective service for all their personal and development needs. TIA has structured this very carefully so the support provided by TIA will be proficient. Today's Bangladeshi community in Greater Manchester is very different from those who arrived as the first wave of migrants. Our Project "the Oral History of Bangladeshis' in Greater Manchester" highlights this progress four generations on. Today, the community is well integrated into mainstream society but inequality and disadvantage in accessing services still exist, that is why TIA exists.

However, over the years, we have had to adapt to the changing needs and expectations of the community. Whereas in the early days, it was about language, access to basic services, and communication issues, today, the challenges are mirroring those experienced by the mainstream communities. Unemployment, drugs, crime, etc are affecting the community. We are working with mainstream agencies in a partnership role to better inform them of the needs and expectations of our still hard-to-reach community. As ever, we work with very limited resources, supporting ever-increasing numbers and higher demands for our services.

TIA's is connected with the worldwide community by Facebook and other social networks. The community benefited from exchanging news and views through these online services. In the past, the TIA has developed two projects in Bangladesh, one in Sylhet and another one in Barishall. We have also plan to do two projects, one is re-housing projects for poor people and another one is to develop a medical college and a hospital in Sylhet.

We are creating a growing number of role models representing diverse fields and are all proud to be British and Bangladeshi. Their success is down to the hard work and dedication of many of our volunteers. More importantly, their success, our success is down to many of the parents and grandparents, respected elders who took part in the Oral History Project, and who are now reaping the benefits of the hard work.
Our young people and community is progressing, moving forward, achieving success, and creating role models for future generations. TIA is proud to lay its part in helping to bring about the small changes that will have a huge impact in the future.

TIA has and continues to work with volunteers to provide most of our services. Encouraging local people in the community to give something back has been our greatest success and this is the most powerful way to show the community that change, and improvements are possible.

1.2 Introduction of the Oral History Project:

The long-term migration has from Bangladesh is a well-known phenomenon. A good number of people who are of Bangladeshi origin now reside in different countries of the world as long-term migrants. Industrialised countries of Europe, North America, and Australia are the most important destinations of these long-term emigrants.

The People of Bangladeshi have made their marks in many fields ranging from economic activities to the academic arena. They have developed successful enterprises. The restaurant industry is one such enterprise that brought long-term emigrant Bangladeshis to the forefront. Due to the hard work done by the Bangladeshis, curry has become the second staple food of the UK.

Along with host countries, Bangladesh has also made significant gains from the long-term immigration of a section of its population. Long-term emigrants played a glorious role during the war of independence of Bangladesh. The continuous flow of remittance is another of their well-recognised contributions. New export markets have opened up for Bangladesh. Bengali ethnic goods, cultural and spiritual materials are being exported to different countries of the world to cater to the demand created by long-term emigrants.

The emigrant population is also showing interest to invest. Regular visits to Bangladesh by the emigrant population play a positive role in developing the economy in general. The UK immigrants Bangladeshis are also getting involved in local and national politics.

This opens new opportunities for influencing public policies in favour of the Bangladeshi community. The emigrant population has certain emotional, social, and cultural requirements for which they want to maintain a certain degree of relationship with Bangladesh. This in many cases results in economic, social, and cultural interactions.

Different studies on migration have shown that the migrant community can work as a bridge between the host (UK) and their home country, and migrants' economic and social interaction can be beneficial for all three parties; the migrant, the host country, and the home country.

The Governments of Bangladesh have gradually realised the importance of its emigrant communities. The seventh parliamentary Government took the most decisive step in this respect and created a separate ministry, the Ministry of Expatriates' Welfare and Overseas Employment, to efficiently manage the migration sector. The Ministry has been entrusted with the duties of managing both long-term and short-term migration.

Since the mid-1970s, the Government of Bangladesh has been involved in regulating and controlling short-term labour migration, long-term migration. However, is a completely new area of Government intervention. The Ministry in this area aims to ensure the well-being of the long-term emigrants, as well as to create space for them to participate in the development process of Bangladesh.

In order to do so, the Government needs to develop a concrete plan of action. Moreover, there hardly exists any systematic information base to plan the sector. There is no information about the nature of emigrant Bangladeshi communities abroad, their professional expertise, and the types of problems they face either in the country of immigration or the country of their origin. Besides, the Government also requires identifying the needs for capacity building of its functionaries for the efficient management of this sector.

Hence, it is important to undertake an in-depth study on the issue to ensure efficient use of the limited resources of the Government. This study is a modest attempt to provide the policymakers, civil society organisations, the private sector, and the emigrant community with the necessary information to develop policies and strategies in this regard. The Long-term emigrant community of Bangladesh is much dispersed.

However, most Bangladeshi immigrants reside in the UK. Due to time and resource constraints, this study was based on the experiences of emigrant Bangladeshis in the UK.

1.3   Objectives:

The objectives of the study can be divided into two parts: policy objectives and, research objectives.
The research objectives of the studies are:

Review existing literature and studies on long-term emigrant Bangladeshis living particularly in Greater Manchester (UK).

Trace the processes of their migration and settlement patterns.

Sketch social, economic, and cultural profiles of emigrant Bangladeshi communities.

Gather data and analyses those for identifying their needs, concerns, and priorities.

Gauge the level and nature of links of such emigrants with Bangladesh, particularly of the first-generation Bangladeshi immigrants.

Assess the scope and the role of immigrant Bangladeshis on the political and economic machinery in formulating policies towards British Bangladeshis.

The policy objectives of the studies are:

Suggest policy measures to the relevant authorities for addressing immediate and long-term issues concerns of the emigrant communities of Bangladeshis living in Greater Manchester.

Suggesting policies and recommendations for the relevant authorities to develop policies and projects for the benefit of the local community.

Recording the history of first-generation Bangladeshi immigrants who migrated to the UK, to share the experience with the wider community and to get benefit from our research.

1.4 Introduction of the Author:

Mustafa Ahmed Mustak

Mr. Mustak is a highly intelligent, educated, and perceptive person. His natural careless, knowledge, and experiences have been of great influence and assistance to the Bangladeshi community which has been recognised and appreciated widely throughout the UK and Bangladesh.

Whilst he was in Bangladesh, he was successfully running 2 businesses with the full assistance of his father and was a news reporter and contributor for the "the Weekly Sylhet Songbad", "Daily Sylheter Dak", "Potrika" and monthly magazine "Tiloth-Thoma". In 1986 he successfully produced a film named "Shuk Duker Pritibi"; he also took an acting role in the film.

Mr. Mustafa came to the UK in 1989 and has made an impact within the various communities through volunteering and in the management of voluntary organisations. He first became involved with the "Tower Hamlets Homeless Families Campaign" in East London. He has contributed to the delivery of the key objectives such as timely re-housing, school admission, and welfare benefits for homeless families. He eventually became one of the management committee members making a direct contribution to the planning and development of the project.

He has also worked with the "Tameside Metropolitan Borough Council" as a housing development officer. Whilst he was working there, he was also working as a tutor at "Mossley Hollins High School" for GCSE students. He worked with the "BACP" in Rochdale as a senior advice worker and worked for the "Glodwick SRB project" in Oldham.

Mustak was actively involved in developing a Credit Union in Hyde and he became the director for the "Hyde Credit Union". He also played a key role as the trustee of "Croft Millennium Trust", which negotiated with Tameside Council for a piece of land in Hyde to develop as a children's play area. This space is being utilised by children and the elderly for socialisation and recreation. He had taken initiative to set up a community learning centre in Hyde by securing funding from National Lottery.

He had done an action research project for Tameside MBC to investigate the employment, business, education, housing, and health of the Hyde and Bangladeshi community. He was also involved in doing the Bangla audio dubbing for a documentary video project called "Catering for whom?" and translated a part of a poetry book called "Untold words" which was published in 1996.

Mustafa was involved in interviewing participants of the oral history project, and he had given support to the volunteers by doing the recordings, editing, transcriptions, translations, and finally the publication of it all. He also used his previous experience in undertaking the research work for this history project had given this book extra strength and added more valuable information for the researcher and the future generation to study this material.
In 2000, Mustak has written & published a history book called "Bangladeshis in Great Britain", particularly for the Hyde Bangladeshi community. He also contributed as an editor of a Bangla literature magazine called "Setu Bandhan" published in March 2002 by the Tigers International Association -TIA. He had published a book called "Life in the UK Test Guide" in 2007; He also published his poetry books "Spondon" & "Chetona" in 2013.

He has taken the leading role to set up several different groups in Hyde, Ashton-u-Lyne, Oldham, Rochdale, and Manchester. These groups are as followed: Shapla Forum (Community consultation group) Surma Bangladeshi Group (Senior citizen group), Job Club (Bangladeshi unemployed group), Bangladesh Mela Steering Group (Arts & culture), Bangladesh Social Club, and Tigers International Association -TIA. Throughout the years he has organised several community events such as seminars, workshops, festivals, and children play schemes, which benefited the Asian communities. In doing so he has given the opportunities to volunteers to develop their various skills including being organised, having leadership, and using teamwork.

In 2004 Mustafa successfully set up an Immigration Law Practice focusing on the UK immigration law in Manchester, Birmingham & London. The practice was well established and busy organisation with offices across the Northwest and London.

He is chief editor of "Probash Barta 24.com" and presenter of PB24TV and hosting various programmes including "community matters", poetry, music, legal advice and so on. The Probash Barta 24.comonline newspaper is aiming to accommodate various topics including health, education, employment, training, business, literature, history, politics, sports for the benefit of the wider community. This publication is targeting the creation of a new audience. Mr. Mustak hosted a programme known as "Community Probin" at ATN Bangla and contributing as a regional reporter for Channel S.

Since 1991, Mustafa has been involved with various organisations such as Manchester TEC, Oldham Business Enterprise, RMBC, Tameside Racial Equality Council (TREC), Oldham Development Agency for Community Action (ODACA) now known as Voluntary Action Oldham - VAO, Manchester Business Link, First Step Project, Stuart Ridgeway, Princes Youth Business Trust, Salford NHS Trust.

Furthermore, he has successfully obtained funding from National Lottery Charities Board, BBC Children in Need, Northwest Arts Board, Princess Youth Business Trust, Tameside MBC, Oldham MBC, Glodwick SRB, Greater Manchester Community Trust, Commonwealth Youth Exchange Council, and BICA for various organisations he worked for.

He seeks truth in every area of his life, whether in learning, discussing values, or relating to his fellow community members and others. He is seen as one of the most distinguished community and social workers in Greater Manchester.

CHAPTER 2 – RESEARCH AND ANALYSIS:

2.1 Analytical Framework:

There are a few analytical perspectives available for explaining the relationship of long-term migrants with their countries of origin and destination. These perspectives, however, mostly reflect the British views. From the perspective of the UK, three concepts are well known.

These are melting pot theory, cultural mosaic theory, and multiculturalism. From the sending country perspective, the brain drain theory is the most well-known. Two other concepts have come into recent usage. These are Diaspora and trans-nationalism. The following section makes a brief discussion on the above concepts and decides on a framework for analysing the first-generation Bangladeshi Immigrants in Greater Manchester, UK.

2.2 Melting Pot, Cultural Mosaic, and Multiculturalism:

The melting pot theory has later been criticised as being both unrealistic and racist. It is argued that this theory focused on the Western heritage and excluded non-European immigrants. Besides, despite its proclaimed "melting" character its results have been assimilationist. The concept of the cultural mosaic is used in the context of the UK. Each immigrant's or family's culture of origin is respected as an independent.

They are not expected to "melt". It also respects immigrant's choice to keep their cultural identity (Willet, 1998). There is hardly any difference in methods they use in creating or moulding the culture of subsequent generations.

Major theorising on long-term migration took place during the 1960s that reflected the concerns of the developing world. Migration under this perspective was generally perceived as a brain drain from the developing world to the developed world. The industrialised countries have been encouraging the migration of particular groups of people from developing countries.

They were the professional and skilled human resources of the countries concerned. The developing states make a huge investment in human resource development with the expectation that such trained manpower will advance the society and economy at large. As education in most of the developing states is highly subsidised, migration of this trained workforce to the developed world is viewed as having a retarding effect on the former.

In recent times, however, long-term migration is being seen from a somewhat different perspective. Some examples are found where a section of them at a certain stage of their life return to their country of origin and contribute positively by using the knowledge and technology learned in the country of immigration. It is in this context that the term brain circulation enters the migration discourse (Naim: 2003)

2.3 Diaspora and Trans-nationalism:

Diaspora is an old term originating from a Greek word. The 'Diaspora' is defined as transnational groups of immigrants living abroad in the host countries but maintaining economic, political, social, and emotional ties with their homeland and with other diasporic communities of the same origin (Sek Pye LIM:2001). Such a view sometimes brought suspicion in some quarters about the ultimate loyalty of the emigrants. Transnationals in this context helped explain the loyalty of the immigrants.

The transnational stresses that migrants can live in two spaces at the same time. They argue that migrants seemed to be continuously negotiating their identities between the context of sending and receiving states (Salazar, 2001). Development in information and communication technologies has enabled migrant groups to keep in contact with their families and friends at home with relative ease. Contemporary processes of global economic, social, and cultural integration are creating transnational communities.

2.4 Source of Information:

For this research, Diaspora has been viewed as communities of migrants settled permanently in and owing allegiance to host countries while at the same time aware of their origin and identity and maintaining varying degrees of linkage with their country of origin and with other diasporic communities of the same origin.

The long-term emigrants from Bangladesh fit in nicely with this concept. The primary allegiance of the long-term emigrant Bangladeshi is of course towards their host country. It is the host country, which benefits the most from the value that is being created by their economic activities. In the receiving countries, the emigrants Bangladeshis also get the opportunity to maximise the return from their skills or enjoy other gains, social or political. Along with this, they pursue a relationship with Bangladesh, to satisfy their social and cultural needs.

Such a relationship in the case of many countries has produced spontaneous economic interactions. When such relationships are institutionalised, they bring benefits to all parties, the sending states, receiving states, and the emigrants. In studying long-term emigrant Bangladeshis, this conceptual framework has been used.

It has been mentioned earlier that the issue of the Bangladeshi Diaspora is one of the least explored areas in the existing migration literature of Bangladesh. Therefore, it was very important to identify different sources for gathering information. The Government, non-Government and private sources of information are identified as follows:

2.4.1 Individual Participants:

Greater Manchester was a boundary to conduct the interviews of Bangladeshi settlers in this area, who arrived in the UK between the 1940s to 1970s (Bangladeshi expatriates). Therefore, field research workers identified people and selected 50 people from Hyde, Ashton-under-Lyne, Oldham, Rochdale, Chester, Salford, and Manchester.

2.4.2 Government:

The departments including the Home Ministry and the Ministry of Foreign Affairs have been identified as potential sources of information.

The Office of the national statistic, UK has been identified as a potential source of information.

All the local authorities (Council) in Greater Manchester have been identified as another source of information.

The Assistant High Commission of Bangladesh located in Manchester was identified as another potential source of information regarding the first-generation Bangladeshi Immigrant (expatriate communities) in the UK.

2.4.3 Academic/Community Based Organisations:

The Bangladeshi Associations located in Greater Manchester were also a good source of information on the nature of emigrants in the UK. Associations of Bangladeshis were also important sources for contacting and interviewing first-generation Bangladeshi Immigrants (expatriates) of different professional and economic backgrounds.

The research institutions like the Manchester Metropolitan University and the Huddersfield University were identified as useful sources of obtaining guidance and advice for conducting this research project.

Some key resource persons were identified to prioritise major issues.

Professor Melanie Tebbutt – Director of the Manchester Centre for Regional History, Manchester Metropolitan University.

Professor Richard Morris OBE, Dr. Robert Light – Centre for visual and Oral History Project, Huddersfield University

Andrew Schofield – Northwest Sound Archive.

2.5   Research Methodology:

In pursuing a study on a new area with limited resources, a comprehensive research methodology needed to be developed. Methodological techniques that were applied in this study are described below.

2.5.1   Gathering of Primary Data:

Given the paucity of information, a methodology has been designed that relies more on the generation of primary data. Greater Manchester was a boundary to conduct the interviews of Bangladeshi settlers in this area, who arrived in the UK between the 1940's to the 1970's (Bangladeshi expatriates). Therefore, field research was conducted in Hyde, Ashton-under-Lyne, Oldham, Rochdale, Salford, Chester, and Manchester.

Most of the first-generation Bangladeshi immigrants (expatriates of the UK) are residing in the area of Greater Manchester. Therefore, in Greater Manchester, six metropolitan Boroughs such as Tameside, Oldham, Rochdale, Manchester, Salford, and Chester were selected as the primary sites for data collection.

Information was gathered at two stages. Firstly, through interviews of key office holders of different associations. Secondly, by interviewing the first-generation Bangladeshi immigrants (expatriates). However, this study did not allow much scope for a broad-based field survey of first-generation Bangladeshi immigrants due to limited resources. Therefore, in-depth interviews of a selected group of emigrants, both male and female, representing various professional, non-professional, and skill categories were conducted.

The fieldwork in Greater Manchester (UK) took place between November 2007 and September 2010. The designated staff of the Tigers International Association – TIA participated in the fieldwork for some time. Their participation convinced the individual first-generation Bangladeshi immigrants (expatriates) about the commitment to take part in the interview. That enabled us to generate primary information.

The interviews took place in a very informal way with their language, so people felt comfortable taking part in the discussion and gave us their version of the story. The interviews were recorded in video format and then transcribed those interviews into Bangla language and then translated into English. Conducting the interviews within the strict schedule was very difficult due to many reasons as individuals were not available or they had some health issues.

All individual participants were informed beforehand about the type of questions the research team would like to ask in the interview. In this study area meetings were conducted with the individuals at their homes.

The press release was sent to print media informing the community about this important piece of work had begun. This initiative of the media resulted in people contacting the researchers and organising meetings in their homes.

A list of key resource persons was prepared before the fieldwork. These people were approached for organising meetings with their respective organisations. Four broad categories of people were covered; the people who have arrived in the UK from the 1940's to the 1970's, people who are involved in community work, people who were involved with the business, and people who had worked within the factories or a different job.

Qualitative statements of the history project were processed manually. Once the first draft of the statement was prepared, then the statements were reviewed by the research team, as the initial translations were carried out by different individuals.

Based on suggestions from the above sources, the final report has been prepared. There are a few limitations of this study. The time limit for fieldwork was short. With the 50% nomination through Bangladeshi Associations, we selected the remaining 50% of people from the local community who worked with us.

2.5.2 Gathering of Secondary Information:

The published materials and research reports that are available in various Government agencies, research institutions, and selected universities in the UK, constituted the most important source of secondary information. The Office for National Statistics (ONS) already has some secondary materials in its collection. Along with these, other secondary materials such as books, journals, and periodicals were collected.

2.5.3 Organisation of the publication of History Book:

To do the publications of the history book, our dedicated volunteers and staff had to undertake the transcriptions of the videos and writing the original scripts which were in Bangla. Then another team of volunteers and staff were involved in doing the translations of the scripts. Finally, the editorial board had done the review of their work and finalised the publication of the book. In addition to this, we dedicated some tasks to the workers to do comprehensive research work to analyse and finalise some of the data and information.

CHAPTER 3: HISTORY & CULTURE

3.1 History of Bangladesh:

Bangladesh is a new state in an ancient land. On the face of it, the recent twists and turns of its history are often inconsistent. It is neither a distant geographical entity nor a well-defined historical unit. Nevertheless, it is the homeland of the ninth-largest nation in the world, whose groupings for a political identity were protracted, intense, and distressing.

The key to these apparent contradictions lies in its history. The word Bangladesh is derived from the cognate "Vanga" to linguists, the roots of the term Vanga may be traced to languages in the adjoining areas. One school of linguists maintains that the word "Vanga" is derived from the Tibetan word "bans" which implies "wet and moist". According to this interpretation, Bangladesh refers to a wetland. Another school believes that the term "Vangla" is derived from Bodo aborigines of Assam words "Bang" and "la", which connote "wide pains".

Geological evidence indicates that much of Bangladesh was formed 1 to 65 million years ago. Human habitation in this region is, therefore, likely to be very old. They are likely to be 10,000 to 15,000 years old.

The history of Bangladesh is as old as it is eventful. In the ancient age, an Austro-Asian race first inhabited this area. Then there were the Dravidians from west India and later the Aryans from Central Asia to establish small settlements. There was also an influx of Mongolians and some Arabs, Persians, Turks, and Afghans.

Bangladesh began the process of peaceful conversion to Islam in the 11th century. By the 14th century, the area was predominantly Muslim, and Muslim rule continued until the British took over after the defeat of the last sovereign ruler Nawab Sirajuddowla, at the Battle of Plassey on 23rd June 1757. The British ruled the sub-continent for 190 years from 1757 to 1947.

During British rule, Bangladesh was a part of the British Indian Provinces of Bengal and Assam. In August 1947, it gained independence from the rest of India and formed a part of Pakistan and was known as East Pakistan. It remained in Pakistan for about 24 years i.e., from 14th August 1947 to 25th March 1971.

After the war of liberation from 25th March to 15th December 1971, Bangladesh emerged as an independent and sovereign Republic on 16th December 1971.

Bangladesh is a unitary, independent, and sovereign country known as the People's Republic of Bangladesh. The official language of Bangladesh is BANGLA. The national flag of the Republic consists of a circle-coloured red throughout its area resting on a bottle green background.

The national emblem of the Republic is the national flower "SHAPLA" (nymphoes nouchali) resting on the water having on each side an ear of paddy and being surmounted by three connected leaves of jute with two stars on each side of the leaves.

The Capital city is DHAKA. The citizens of Bangladesh are known as BANGLADESHI.

3.2 Architecture:

Factors of climate and geography and indigenous building materials such as timber and bamboo conditioned the development of architecture in Bangladesh. The predominantly brick tradition in architecture can be called its own.

Both the pre-Muslim temple and monastic architectures followed an indigenous style through strongly imbued with the contemporary foreign pattern. The Mughals brought about a fundamental change by totally discarding the traditional terracotta art of the region.

At the turn of the nineteenth century, a new hybrid of Mughal and European styles emerged. Modern architecture, characterised using reinforced concrete for multi-storeyed buildings with straight horizontal and vertical lines dominating the elevation, appeared after the partition of the sub-continent in 1947.

3.3 Literature:

More than 95% of the people speak Bangla, which originated from the Eastern Prakrit of the Indo-Aryan family of languages. Early Bangla in its lyrical form, originated in the seventeenth century.

Michael Madhusudan
Datta

Sarat Chandra
Chattopadhyay

Rabindranath
Tagore

Kazi Nazrul Islam

Jashim Uddin

Since the early decades of this century, modern Bangla literature has swept into the mainstream of world culture through the works of such geniuses as Michael Madhusudan Dutta, Sarat Chandra Chattopadhyay, Mir Musharraf Hussain, Kazi Abdul Wadood, Rabindranath Tagore, and rebel poet Kazi Nazrul Islam. While poet Jasmuddin's austere lyrical anecdotes depicting rural life kept alive the link with the toiling masses.

3.4 Art:

Bangladesh has a rich tradition of painting and terracotta art. Episodes from mythologies, legends, and love lures, above all, natures' beauty found artistic expression in terracotta, pottery, clay dolls, handicrafts, and embroidery. Artists like Zainul Abedin, Qamrul Hasan, Anwarul Haque, Saifuddin Ahmed, Shafiqul Amin, Rashid Chowdhury, and SM Sultan pioneered Modern painting. Zainul Abedin earned worldwide fame by his stunning sketches of the Bengal Famine in 1943. Most of our modern painters are steeped in this tradition.

| Zainul Abedin | Qamrul Hasan | Shaifuddin Ahmed |
| Rashid Chowdhury | SM Sultan | Shafiqul Amin |

Dhaka has turned into an important centre of art in the region through the regular holding of the Asian Art Biennial.

3.5 Music:

The rich tradition of music in Bangladesh can be divided into three distinctive categories: - classical, folk, and modern. The tradition of classical music, whether vocal or instrumental, is rooted in the history of this sub-continent.

Folk music, nurtured through the ages by village bands, is the most popular form of music in Bangladesh. The best-known forms are Bhatiali, Ba-ul, Marifoti, Murshidi, and Bhawaiya.

Modern Bengali music originated from two distinct schools. The first is essentially a blend of East and West initiated by Rabindranath Tagore; the second experimented with the synthesis of classical, folk, and Middle Eastern Strains, which was spearheaded by rebel poet Kazi Nazrul Islam. The contemporary adherents of both the schools have been widening their depth and vista with new experiments.

3.6 Dance:

Dancing in Bangladesh draws freely on the sub-continental classical forms as well as the folk, tribal, ballet, and Middle Eastern strains. Of the tribal dances, particularly popular are Manipuri and Santal.

3.7 Drama:

Theatre in Bangladesh has a tradition, which is more than a century old. In the early days, open-air theatrical performances, known as Jatra (rural operetta), used to be held on festive occasions. Popular love lore's, historical or legendary, acts of valour heroes against invading forces, and mythological anecdotes alongside the legends of the Arabian Persian Nights provided the basic themes of popular Jatra plays which still the most popular form of most entertainment in the country.

3.8. Religion:

Bangladesh is traditionally a land of communal harmony. The constitution guarantees full and equal religious freedom to all communities. The government has set up different trusts for the welfare of Hinduism, Buddhism, and Christianity. The religious profile of the population is Islam 90.4%, Hinduism 8.5%, Buddhism 0.6%, Christianity 0.4%, and others (such as Animists and non-religious) 0.1% as per the 2011 census. The majority of the Muslims are Sunni consisting of 95% of the Muslim population, and the remaining are Shi'a and other sects.

Hindus constituted 18.5% of the population in 1961, but their population declined significantly during the Bangladesh Liberation War due to the 1971 Bangladesh atrocities carried out by the Pakistan Army. As a result, millions of Hindus fled to India and their population in Bangladesh fell to 13.5% by 1974. Since then, the Hindu population has not grown as much as the Muslim population.

3.8.1 Islam:

Bangladesh is the second-largest Muslim country in the world. About 86.6% of its 120 million people are Muslim. Dhaka, the capital, is known as the city of mosques. It has nearly 2,000 mosques. There are about 200,000 mosques all over Bangladesh.

By the end of the first century of Islam, the Arab traders and Muslim missionaries brought Islam to this deltaic region. Its message of equality and fraternity drew the masses toward it. Embracing Islam meant salvation from social tyranny and elevation in social status. Islam came as a relieving force in which the people found an easy opening to success. Perhaps because of this Islam is so deep-rooted in this region.

3.8.2 Hinduism:

In Bangladesh, 8.5% of the whole country belongs to the Hindu community. After the partition of India in 1947, many Hindu landlords and members of the educated middle class left for India from this part of Pakistan. The Hindus in Bangladesh today are active in agriculture, fishing, business, teaching, journalism, engineering, medicine and law, politics, etc. Many Hindus are also employed in government and autonomous bodies.

It is said the Hindus worship many gods and goddesses. The puja (worship) of Brahma, Vishnu, Shiva, Durga, Kali, Laksmi, and Saraswati are more popular. Though they worship many gods and goddesses Hindus do not worship many creators. In the Vedas, it is said that the different gods are manifestations of one Supreme Being.

3.8.3 Buddhism:

Scholars are divided in their opinion about the origin of Buddhism in Bangladesh, Its influence here, as in other parts of the sub-continent, is generally attributed to Emperor Asoka, the greatest patron of Buddhism, and it is believed that Buddhism came to Bangladesh in the third century BC. But the proximity of this country to Magadha (Present Bihar), the birthplace of Buddhism, suggests earlier contacts, which seems to support pre-Asokan traditions.

Thus, Buddhism found a strong base in Bangladesh from the very beginning and flourished in many parts of the country afterward during the reigns of the Buddhist Khadga, Deva, Pala, and Chandra kinds till the twelfth century AD.

Indeed, in the whole of the sub-continent, it is on the soil of Bangladesh that the religion of the Tathagata found its last shelter and took firm roots.

The Buddhist population of Bangladesh is approximately 70,000, which is less than 1% of the total population. They comprise Barua Buddhists living in the plainlands and Maghs living in south Chittagong and Khepupara of Barisal and the tribes of the Chittagong Hill Tracts.

3.8.4   Christianity:

The Portuguese missionaries brought the Christian faith to Bengal in the early sixteenth century. The oldest church situated in the city of Dhaka, dates back to 1677. There are no less than 225 churches in the country. The number of native-born Christians in Bangladesh is about half a million. About half of them are tribal's. The religious leadership is entirely in the hands of the local people. They are well integrated into the mainstream of society. For centuries they have lived together in peace and harmony with the people of other religions.

3.9   Customs and Traditions of Bangladesh:

Bangladesh has its customs and traditions-some rooted in its prehistory and others, relatively recent. The indigenous customs, being an integral part of the life cycle of the people, have a universal appeal. Bangladesh has been predominantly agricultural ever since man arrived there and started domesticating animals and practicing rudimentary forms of tillage. The indigenous customs have therefore grown around agricultural practices.

3.9.1 Naming Ceremony:

The birth of a child is celebrated with the distribution of sweets, Swadesh, or Sandesh pita. The naming ceremony, akika, amongst the Muslims, is observed with a feast and invitees bring the presents.

3.9.2 Nabanna (New Rice):

The festival of the next harvest takes place in the Bangla month of Agrahayon (Nov-Dec). People in the rural areas celebrate the harvesting of the corn as farmers come back home with lots of golden paddy on their heads ringing like new bells. In the yard, the cattle go around and around, thrashing the paddy separating it from the stalks. The women make pita, cheer, and serve all the neighbors, there is joy everywhere.

3.9.3 Pahela Baishakh (Bengali New Year):

Bengali's New Year's Day is indigenous and has been part of its folk tradition for a long time. The day starts with the partaking of a heavy breakfast of cheera, ghur, and yogurt. The fairs take place every sort, food of every variety and sweets of endless kinds. Businessmen and traders observe this day with due solemnity. They start a new cash register, which is known as halkhata. In the cities, there are cultural functions and Baishakhi Mela (fairs) take place.

3.10. Religious Customs:

3.10.1 Akika (Islamic):

After the birth of a child, Muslim people sacrifice an animal in the name of Allah. When a boy is born two goats are sacrificed, for a girl on a goat is sacrificed and the meat is distributed to the poor, relatives, and neighbours. The people who can afford to buy a goat will do the Akika. In Hadith, Hazrat Mohammed (SAW) said the child or his parent who has not done the Akika and if the child has died, at the time of Akhirat, he or she could not request anything from Allah for his or her parents. Therefore, Imam Shafei, Ahmed, and Malik (RA) Akika emphasised Sunnah and according to Imam Abu Haifa (RA), Akika was less emphasized Sunnah.

3.10.2 Mussalmani or Khatna (Circumcision):

This is common among Muslims; it is an occasion of happiness. In the rural areas, the child is given a ride on the palanquin or a horse or donkey before he is brought before the hajam (the men who do the operation).

3.10.3 After Death:

The Muslims and Christians bury the dead body, the Hindus perform the cremation. Muslims observe a Kul-khani (distribution of food) after the third day of death, while a Chehlam (plenty of food for the poor & relatives) is held on the Fortieth day. The Hindus, likewise, hold a Sraddha (respect) as the sons of the deceased shave of their hair in mourning.

3.11. Religious Celebrations:

3.11.1 Shob-e-Barat:

It means the night of fortune. The Muslims believe that on this night Allah determines human destiny for the rest of the year. Most Muslims spend the nights doing prayers and Zikirs hoping Allah would forgive all the people. This takes place on the fourteenth of Shaban according to the Arabic calendar.

3.11.2 Ramadan:

The ninth month of the Islamic calendar, a full month of fasting for all Muslim adults and it is compulsory for everyone. No food is allowed during the day from sunrise to sunset. It teaches us fellow-feeling, sacrifice, and temperance and most of all restrain. People pay Zakath (a compulsory contribution to the poor).

3.11.3 Shob-e-Qadar:

Shob means night and Shob-e-Qadar is a night of special significance. It takes place on the night of the 27th day of Ramada. The holy Quran is revealed on this night but according to the hadiths, there is a lack of certainty about the precise date of this occasion. The hadiths point at the odd night after the 20th Ramadan, namely the 21st, 23rd, 25th & 27th. Bangladeshi people observe the 27th Ramadan as a Shob-e-Qadar and they spend all night praying to Allah.

3.11.4 Eid-ul-Fitr:

Eid-ul-Fitr comes at the end of the month-long fasting during Ramadan and the sighting of the new moon of Shawal, the 10th of the Arabic calendar. The Muslim people wear new clothes, eat delicious dishes and male members go to the Edgah or the mosque to make a special prayer. The people embrace each other, and the poor are given Fitra (a certain amount of money per head). The people enjoy the occasion most as they visit their friends and relatives.

3.11.5 Hajj (Pilgrimage to Makkah):

Hajj is the Fifth important pillar of Islam, which has got a historical background, without which one cannot fully understand and appreciate its importance and real objective.

The pilgrimage to Makkah, the Hajj is an obligation only for those who are physically and financially able to do so. Nevertheless, over two million people go to Makkah each year from every corner of the globe providing a unique opportunity for those of different nationalities to meet one another.

The annual hajj begins in the 12th month of the Islamic lunar year. Pilgrims wear special clothes: simple garments that strip away distinctions of class and culture so that all stand before Allah.

The rights of the Hajj, which are of Abrahamic origin, include going around the Ka'bah seven times, and going seven times between the hills of Safa and Marwa as did Hagar (Abraham's wife) during her search for water. The pilgrims later stand together on the wide plains of Arafat (a large expanse of desert outside Makkah) and join in prayer for Allah's forgiveness, in what is often thought as a preview of the Day of Judgment.

The close of the Hajj is marked by a festival, the Eid-ul-Azha, which is celebrated with prayers and the exchange of gifts in Muslim communities everywhere. The Eid-ul-Fitr is a festive day celebrating the end of Ramadan.

3.11.6 Eid-ul-Azha:

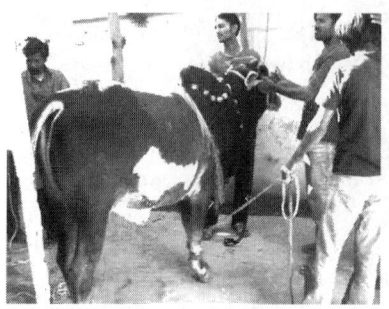

Eid-ul-Azha takes place on the 10th of Zilhaj; it is the next important occasion for the Muslims. Those who can afford it, go to Makkah to perform Hajj. But most people celebrate it with devotion offering prayers and the sacrifice of either a cow or a goat. This is done in memory of Hazrat Ibrahim (SM) who out of love for Allah, was about to sacrifice his dearest son Ismail (SM) but ended up sacrificing as stood blindfolded, a sheep. People distribute meat amongst the poor and the poor relations and there is joy and happiness all around. This too is observed as an occasion of national importance.

3.11.7 Eid-e-Miladunnabi:

This signifies the birth anniversary of Hazrat Mohammed (SM), the prophet of Islam. He was born on Monday 12th of Rabiul Awwal, an Arabic lunar month, In 570 AD. The Muslim of the sub-continent celebrates the birth anniversary of the prophet with great respect, enthusiasm, and passion for several days including the 12th.

3.11.8 Durga Puja:

The Hindu has several religious festivals amongst which the Durga Puja is the most important. The Hindu localities either collectively or individually have the images of goddess Durga killing Mahishasura made in clay, daub the idols in paint, and make them wear bright clothes. This festival starts in Aswin when the moon appears in the sky. On the 10th day, the image is immersed in water, usually in a river or a pond then the devotees come back home. This is a great occasion of joy and merriment for Hindus. They wear new clothes and lots of dainty dishes are prepared on this occasion.

3.11.9 Christmas:

In tune with the rest of the world, the Christians of Bangladesh observe their most important religious festival, X-mas, on the 25th of December to celebrate the birth of Jesus Christ.

3.12 Shaheed Day (Language Day):

On 21st February 1952, the youths (especially the students) rose in protest the imposition of Urdu as the only state language of Pakistan. This was taken as a conspiracy against the Bangla culture and as the students brought out a procession in violation of official prohibitor order, the Police fired on the demonstrators killing many of the students and also killing some members of the public. Barkat, Salam, Rafiq, Jabber, and many unknown others had lost their lives.

After Independence February 21st had been officially declared the Shaheed day (the martyrs' day), also called Omar Ekushey (the immortal 21st). The day observed with great solemnity, beginning from midnight. Streams of people come and pass the steps of Shaheed Minar laying wreaths on the steps.

The UNESCO has proclaimed February 21st as the International Mother Language Day to be observed globally in recognition of the sacrifices of the martyrs for establishing the rightful place of Bangla. The proclamation came in the form of a resolution unanimously adopted at the plenary of the UNESCO at its headquarters in Paris in November 1999. In this resolution, UNESCO said the 21st of February should be proclaimed the International Mother Language Day throughout the world to commemorate the martyrs who sacrificed their lives on this very day in 1952.

The Bangladesh Government initiated this resolution. It is a great tribute and glowing homage paid by the international community to the language martyrs of Bangladesh. The genesis of the historic Languages Movement ensued that since September 1947 the students in the vanguard would be backed by intellectuals and cultural activities. The patriotic elements were the first spurt of the Bengali nationalistic upsurge culminating in the sanguinary events of February 21st, 1952, and finally leading to the Liberation War in 1971.

The sacrifice of the martyrs received global recognition, and this is a rare honour for Bangladeshis. This recognition was used to promote the dissemination of mother tongues will not only encourage linguistic diversity and multilingual education. It is also developing fuller awareness about linguistic and cultural traditions throughout the world, and inspire solidarity based on understanding, tolerance, and dialogue.

In the new millennium, about 188 countries around the world had observed 21st February as International Mother Language Day. The history of 21st February has thus assumed a new dimension. The sacrifice of Rafiq, Salam, Jabbar, Barkat, and other martyrs as well as those tortured and repressed by the then authoritarian government of Pakistan for Campaigning the cause their mother-tongue had received now a glorious and new recognition by November 1999 resolution of the UNESCO.

3.13 Independence & National Day:

Following the Pakistani army crackdown on 25th March 1971, the independence of Bangladesh was declared on March 26th. Since then the day is observed as Independence and National day.

3.14 The Victory Day:

On 16th December 1971, the Pakistan army, an estimated 90,000 surrendered to the allied forces. The valiant freedom fighters entered the city of Dhaka with arms in their hands. As they marched along the streets, the people welcomed them with rejoicing. The jubilant crowd stood by the Pakistani army marched in silence with their heads drooping low. The day is observed with due solemnity-the first rays of morning sun being heralded with 31 gunshots.

3.15 Conclusion:

There are also other public holidays are observed on the following occasions: May Day: 1st May, Buddha Purnima, Juma's-tul-bida. The dates these occasions are determined are according to the sightings of the moon. Official holidays are observed on the following occasions under executive order of government: Shob-e-Barat, Shob-e-Qadar, Asura (10th Muharram, the first month of Hijri, Islamic calendar year), and 3 days each of the two Eid occasions.

In Britain we observed the following days, such as Ramadan, two Eid days, Shob-e-Barat, Shob-e-Qadar, Durga Puja, National day, Independence Day, Language Day etc.

CHAPTER 4 - Bangladeshis in English law

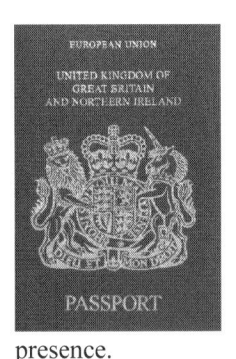

4.1 Abstract:

This article begins with a conceptualisation, in legal-pluralist and agency-oriented terms, of the legal implications of the Bangladeshi presence in Britain. It then examines how immigration restrictions, introduced particularly in the 1980s, were aimed at preventing the settlement of Bangladeshis. There is then a discussion of how some concrete legal problems have been considered in actual court decisions. The article thereby considers the extent to which English law maintains a largely ethnocentric perspective vis-à-vis the Bangladeshi presence.

4.2 The interplay of legal systems or Bangladeshi legal pluralism:

The explanation as to why the Bangladeshi presence in Britain has hardly made a dent in British legal consciousness lies with the nature of and the presuppositions of that which operates within the system. What are these factors then? First, one can point to the predominant fiction that the state's law is at the centre of things and can control and police all aspects of social life within any of the communities that make up contemporary Britain.

The state legal system is largely seen as the property of only some of its social components. A situation of repression (Glenn 2000: 50-53) of other legal orders is therefore in place at all levels, despite a rhetorical recognition by government officers that Britain today is a multicultural society.

The fact of a plural social base is not deemed to require the pluralisation of the official legal system. Rather, there remains the expectation that various others must assimilate to the norms of the majority as a condition of legal protection. Thus, the state law presents a system of 'ethnic penalties' (Modood and Berthoud 1997: 144-145), such that the more 'ethnic' one is seen to be, the more the likelihood of marginalisation or penalisation.

Bangladeshis do not just follow English law upon arrival in Britain, and much less so do they follow English law in Bangladesh, as proponents of the common law's triumph over non-Western legal cultures would have it. We do not know as much as we should about the legal system of Bangladesh. However, its basic setup seems to resemble other South Asian legal systems, with which it also shares a common history in several ways (Monsoor 1999: 59-120).

A key point for us is that the state is a relatively distant phenomenon in psychological terms. It is modeled on the Asian (and African) paradigm of a 'soft state' which, while formally superior, is not interested in dictating the terms of everyday life and law for most people (Menski 2000: 11).

Another key distinguishing feature is the place of personal laws in South Asian legal systems. Thus we find that it is officially recognised that different religious or tribal communities will follow their law systems in matters of family, property, and religion - accordingly the state gets involved in administering Muslim law, Hindu law, and so on.

However, in Bangladesh, this system has come under tension with the twin drives for 'Islamisation' and uniformisation (Menski and Rahman 1988, Menski 1997: 18-23).

It would still appear though that, in contrast to the Western model, South Asian legal systems allow a wide scope for the operation of personal law systems, as well as facilitating their official recognition. These differences in understanding the place of the state in the context of its social framework have a crucial role to play in conceptualizing the transplantation of Bangladeshi legal culture in Britain, and they are arguably key determinants in its cognitive interaction with English law.

With the migration to Britain, one can expect that legal patterns that are followed at the personal level are continued unless we make the very unsound assumption that all one's cultural baggage gets lost on the flight to Britain! We, therefore, find that there is the transplantation of Bangladeshi, predominantly Sylhetis legal culture to the bideshi setting.

With the earlier stages of male-dominated migration from Bangladesh, some bideshi habits may have been adopted and there is some evidence in the reported cases that some of these men had got into relationships with local white women.

However, with the arrival of families in more recent decades, we will probably have seen the hardening of societal structures in all sorts of ways (Ballard 1994: 14-18). We will therefore see quite different stages of legal reconstruction and interaction on the road to the establishment of desh bidesh, to adapt Ballard's (1994) formulation, desh pardesh (see already Gardner 1993).

At this stage, it is worth emphasizing that theorizing and fieldwork about the ethnic minority presence in the UK have already moved on despite official dogmas about the respective place of state and society as well as inherent cultural biases. Thus, we already have some material that argues for the recreation of South Asian legal cultures in diasporic contexts (Chiefly, Menski 1993).

For Bangladeshis, the material on Muslim law, or 'angrezi shariat' (Pearl and Menski 1998, Menski 2001) is most relevant, given the overwhelming concentration of Muslims among this group. The concept of angrezi shariat, an Urdu term meaning British Muslim law (ingreji shoriyot in Bangla/Sylheti), is understood as the Muslim legal cultures recreated within the British setting.

I do not see this as the introduction of the textual or doctrinal sharia, even though attention generally tends to focus on this due to prevailing ideological predispositions. It should rather be seen as the more or less conscious process of developing a living law in the Diaspora.

Thus it is that Ballard (nd) argues for greater attention to be paid, not to the concepts of the doctrinal shari'a, but to everyday notions of rivaz (rewaj in Bangla/Sylheti) on which maintenance of honour is crucially predicated.

It could also incorporate adaptations to English legal requirements such as the registration of marriages. A thoroughly hybrid process is therefore presented, and it is evident that all Muslim communities have been engaged in this process to some degree, the Sylhetis no less.

Due to this process being a dynamic one,(Yilmaz 1999) it means that actual fieldwork knowledge is required to appreciate how the culture in the country of origin has adapted to their new setting. Ethnographers, and sometimes even lawyers in practice, are better placed here than legal academics it seems.

What is the status of this emergent Muslim law then? While there were demands in the 1970s from Muslim spokesmen that the state recognises sharia'sofficially, these demands have not been met (Poulter 1990). Muslims have also been campaigning for recognition under the anti-discrimination and blasphemy laws, but these more limited demands have also been pushed away by a state that has been making confident strides towards secularism for decades now.

This form of secularism is not the Indian form of equidistance to all faiths but, drawing on liberal answers to intra-European religious conflicts, demands the 'privatization' of religion. Some concessions, particularly at the local level (Nielsen 1988, 1992, Shah 1994) on issues such as education, mosque building, and slaughter regulations are granted, however, and this probably remains the most viable strategy for obtaining recognition at present (Yilmaz 2000).

According to the classification that we met earlier, therefore, Muslim law, whether in doctrinal form or - much more relevant - in the sense of a living legal system has been pushed firmly into the 'unofficial' sphere. There is not much likelihood that this general position will change soon given serious and no doubt culturally loaded reservations in the West about the compatibility of Muslim laws with human rights norms (Poulter 1990, 1998).

The Muslim response meanwhile seems to have turned to the development of dispute resolution fore as a parallel non-state court system that demonstratively illustrates that the English legal system offers inadequate protective mechanisms (Badawi 1995, Carroll 1997, Pearl and Menski 1998: 77-80, 393-398, Shah-Kazemi 2001, Yilmaz 2001).

4.2.1 Immigration restrictions: preventing the establishment of desh bidesh:

Before going on to examine some of the recent almost contemporaneously decided cases, it may be useful to examine the immigration law response to the prospect of Bangladeshi settlement in Britain. The immigration system is, after all, where much of the legal encounter between Bangladeshis and the English law has been taking place in the last two decades.

The reasons are obvious to ethnographers who have noticed that the establishment of desh bidesh, and thus the regrouping of families in Britain, took place at a later stage for Sylhetis than it did for the other South Asian groups from India or Pakistan.

There was thus a shift from the men's 'international commuter' lifestyle to the arrival of wives and children from the 1970s, peaking in the 1980s, but continuing through the 1990s (Ballard 1994: 20, Gardner and Shukur 1994:

150, Gardner 1995: 114-121, Eade, Vamplew and Peach 1996: 151, Juss 1997: 47-48).

If the decision to reunite families was at least in part motivated by a strategy to avoid waiting for a time when controls would get even stricter, as Gardner and Shukur (1994: 150) indicate, the immigration law system had, by the mid-1980s, fine-tuned its restrictive machinery against South Asian settlement such that Bangladeshis found themselves experiencing its worst aspects.

Indeed, from the mid-1980s we find that restrictions were tightened further specifically in response to Bangladeshi regrouping in Britain. Thus, in August 1985, the Immigration Rules that spouses and fiancées were required to satisfy before obtaining entry clearance were changed so that those applying to enter had to also satisfy the authorities that there would be no recourse to public funds (Sachdeva 1993: 93-100).

This also coincided with the gradually worsening economic position of Bangladeshi men because of de-industrialization in sectors where they were over-represented (Gardner 1995: 48). Many men could still claim exemption from the application of these requirements, however, as they had been working in Britain since before the Immigration Act of 1971.

A clause had been inserted into this Act guaranteeing Commonwealth men who had settled in Britain prior to 1973 that their conditions for a family reunion would be no worse. The full impact of the Rule changes was therefore not evident immediately.

A visa requirement imposed in the autumn of 1986 for visitors from Bangladesh, Pakistan, India, Ghana, and Nigeria effectively came to strictly control travel to Britain, and it had its impact even on those dependants with a claim to British citizenship (Joint Council for the Welfare of Immigrants 1987, Drabu and Bowen 1989, see further below).

The most serious attack on Bangladeshi families came about in the Immigration Act of 1988, however, and Gardner (1995: 48-49) has rightly observed its crucial importance: 'British Bengali men who did not bring their wives and children to the UK in the 1970s may now find themselves embroiled in complicated and expensive legal wrangling, which may take years to resolve, especially since the Immigration Act 1988 now means that their dependents are no longer guaranteed entry.

Countless trips may have to be made to the British High Commission in Dhaka by family members in Bangladesh. Sometimes by the time a case is processed, the conditions of entry are no longer valid. Many rural Sylhetis, like ordinary people in the UK, have only a vague idea of the immigration laws, and none at all of their rights.

The documentary evidence which is acceptable in British courts simply does not exist in rural Bangladesh, for few people know their exact age, let alone have a birth certificate to prove it. The skill of a families' lawyer may well tip the scales in deciding who gets their entry and who does not, and it is the poorer and less well-connected who inevitably lose out.'

This Act did away with the above-mentioned guarantee in the 1971 Act thereby allowing the subjection of Bangladeshis to the stringent and ever more demanding requirements of the Immigration Rules on family reunion. It is, therefore, no coincidence that a huge number of refusals have been made under the public funds' criteria since then.

This is attested to by the fact that public funds cases constitute a large proportion of the load dealt with by the Immigration Appeal Tribunal (Gillespie 1992, McKee 1995, Hussein and Sedona 1996, Wray and Quorum 1999).

The 1988 Act also attempted to neutralize another trump card in Bangladeshi hands. Many South Asian men, Bangladeshis (formerly East Pakistanis) being the most important group here, who came to work in the UK in the earlier periods of post-war migration, acquired a right of abode under the 'partiality' provisions of the Immigration Act 1971.

While South Asian men could not generally establish such a right through ancestral connections or birth in the UK, many were able to do so after five years of residence in the UK, or by registering in the UK as citizens of the UK and colonies (CUKCs) as Gardner and Shukur (1994: 150) have indicated. Importantly, under the partiality provisions, such men could also pass a right of abode on to their wives, including second wives, and children who therefore enjoyed an unfettered right to enter the UK. Further, the children of partial men who had registered themselves as CUKCs became entitled to claim the status of British citizens upon the coming into force of the British Nationality Act 1981.

They could therefore travel to the UK without the need for certificates of entitlement, even on Bangladesh passports, and without being subject to immigration control (see in detail Fransman 1986, Fransman 1989: 210-231). The key events that culminated in the 1988 Act being passed again reinforce the impression that the main target of control was family members from Bangladesh. Fransman (1989: 215) recounts the cumulative effect of the 1986 and 1988 legal changes:

'The Bangladeshi British citizens by descent began to arrive in 1985 and during 1986 the numbers increased substantially. However, as of 16th October 1986, the UK government made Bangladeshis visa nationals. As a matter of law, those claiming British citizenship by descent did not require visas but the airlines, fearful of financial penalties, simply refused to carry any Bangladesh Passport holder without a visa. The result was that in all but a few isolated cases the flow of claimants from Bangladesh was halted.

'The government, however, was not satisfied with a mere de facto prevention of direct arrivals of claimants of British citizenship by descent. The introduction of visas may have placed a hurdle in the path of claimants wishing to travel direct to the UK but did not affect their legal right to do so. Accordingly, after the 1987 election, the government announced its intention to amend the law and so to extinguish the statutory entitlement.'

Thus, the 1988 Act (in section 3(1)) required all claimants to the right of abode or British citizenship to establish that status by obtaining a certificate of entitlement or a British Passport when seeking to enter the UK. This provision obviated the risk of claimants to entry simply arriving at a British port, and rather attempted to ensure that controls were applied at diplomatic posts abroad where any adverse publicity could be avoided.

The 1988 Act also had specific implications for those in polygamous marriages. Some of the earlier immigration case law seems to indicate, at best, an ambivalent official attitude to the recognition of polygamous marriages, and a refusal to allow family reunion could often result even though the persons involved had always considered themselves married under their law.

The 1988 Act and accompanying Immigration Rule changes then introduced a prohibition on the entry of a polygamous married wife where another wife had already been admitted to Britain. This can also be read as a direct attack on Bangladeshi families as the practice of polygamy seems to be having been most prevalent with this group as compared to other South Asians.

Although not significant in terms of overall numbers, these restrictions were also indicative of the fact that the UK legal system was prepared to tolerate the separation of families and mothers from their children, ironically as a way of signalling its civilization superiority (Shah 2002).

As discussed further below such posturing has led to the downgrading of the rights of Bangladeshi children too, who are now deemed illegitimate by English law. A more general point that can be made about the immigration restrictions is that, not only are they aimed at curbing the settlement of Bangladeshis in Britain, but how particular legal conflicts are handled shows much evidence of ethnocentric assumptions in full play within English law. This then has its function in signalling to Bangladeshis that assimilation to dominant norm systems is expected.

4.3 Bangladeshis in English law: a case study in legal ethnocentrism:

If we take the two elements identified earlier - of state centrism and ethnocentrism - together we find that there is ample scope for the dismissal, marginalization, or distortion of Bangladeshi legal culture within English legal fore. On the other hand, we can also find at least some evidence that English judges cannot escape from having to grapple with evidence of Bangladeshi legal reconstruction in Britain despite the official mono-culturalist policy.

Here I want to present evidence from three reported cases to show how these patterns work themselves out in concrete situations. All three cases are linked to the extent that they all deal with the issue of marriage albeit in different contexts, and all three are also, directly or indirectly, concerned with the status of children of the marriages. One concerns the recognition of a long-standing marriage in the absence of evidence of registration or indisputable documentary evidence.

The second is concerned with the consequences of a polygamous marriage for the status of children. The third, which is discussed in a separate section considering the challenging issues it raises, concerns the dreaded mixed marriage and the question of renaming and circumcising the child once the couple has split up.

4.3.1 Sanctity of marriage or over-reliance on kagzi evidence?

In our first case, R (Shamsun Nahar) v Social Security Commissioners (21 December 2001, QBD (Admin Ct), [2001] EWHC Admin 1049), the underlying question was whether the applicant was entitled to a widow's pension as the surviving wife of a Bangladeshi man.

There was some evidence that she had already fought a long legal battle with the immigration authorities to obtain a certificate of entitlement to the right of abode based on her marriage. Her initial appeal against refusal of a certificate was allowed but then, on further appeal by the entry clearance officer, the matter was remitted by the Immigration Appeal Tribunal (IAT) to another adjudicator who also allowed the appeal.

The IAT refused leave to appeal further, and the applicant finally arrived in the UK with her son. Throughout the immigration proceedings, the validity of the marriage, which had taken place 'under Muslim tradition and practice' in (what was then) East Pakistan in 1952, was accepted. Also, a document described as a 'marriage deed' had been accepted as valid.

The 'marriage deed' was produced before the Social Security Appeal Tribunal on appeal. The document was referred to a 'document examination officer' within the Department of Social Security. He believed that it was highly unlikely that the marriage deed was issued in 1952. Munby J's judgment then sets out what followed:

'On 27 February 1998, the Social Security Appeal Tribunal refused the claimant's appeal, having found on the balance of probabilities that it had not been established that a valid marriage had been contracted between the [claimant] and Abdul Kadir [her deceased husband]. The Tribunal's full reasons were issued on 1 June 1998. Referring to the expert's opinion the Tribunal described the marriage deed as a suspect. The Tribunal concluded on the balance of probabilities that the marriage deed was a forgery.'

The challenge before Munby J then concentrated on the extent to which the social security appeals proceedings ought to have followed the findings as to validity in the immigration proceedings. It was held that there was no such obligation on them, and the judgment is an excellent review of authorities on this and related points. The judge held that even when a party has satisfied one government department of the existence of a certain relationship, other departments may lawfully reopen the issue of validity.

It is common practice for people to obtain secondary documentation to show that the relevant relationship exists when such a need arises. While such documents can never be absolute proof that the relationship claimed exists, neither should it have been assumed that if the documents were not drafted at the time of the relationship's coming into being (for example at the time of a marriage ceremony) that they are necessarily invalid.

Munby J did recognize in the judgment that: 'The claimant thus finds herself in an unenviable and invidious position and, I do not doubt, one which seriously affects her standing in and treatment by her community. As [her counsel] points out, the effect of the Commissioners' decision is to brand her son M as illegitimate.'

Despite this acknowledgment, no significant efforts seem to have been made to satisfy any doubts about the relationships through appropriate means. If the validity of the marriage were at issue, then other rules could have been used.

This must be assumed to be more than an isolated case as Pearl and Menski (1998: 171) have commented: 'In quite a few cases, absence of witnesses or more generally lack of documentation of a Muslim marriage entered into in South Asia has been an issue for the determination before the British courts and tribunals. While the South Asian courts ... lean in favour of recognizing such marriages as valid, European judges appear to need constant reminders of the existence of a strong presumption in favour of marriage in Muslim law.'

Crucially, it does not appear that this was picked up by the lawyers arguing the case and they managed to divert the issue by getting the judge to decide on one of the finer points of English administrative law. In doing so, they missed the essential issue, as did Munby J himself despite recognizing that a finding of invalidity would have undesirable consequences for the applicant and her son. Not only would the decision leave her worse off in financial terms, but English law would also be making allegations of Zina (Jina in Bangla/Sylheti) against her and leaving the status of her son in question.

4.3.2 Questioning the legitimacy of children:

As mentioned above, the English (and Scottish) attitude to the recognition of polygamous marriage has long been ambiguous if not altogether hostile. This hostility has not been sustainable over the long term because courts were inevitably placed in a position of having to decide on the consequences especially when matrimonial relief was sought.

In the early post-war decades, the judicial response was pragmatic but still ethnocentric - convert the marriage to a monogamous one mentally and then provide relief. In the early 1970s however, legislation was specifically passed to allow courts to provide relief in polygamous marriages that had broken down.

At the same time, in a thorough assimilationist move, it was stipulated that no marriage celebrated in England and Wales could be polygamous, and the marriages of English domiciled men were void if contracted in polygamous form (Matrimonial Causes Act 1973, section 11). English law was thus attempting to assert control over non-European men here.

Read literally, the provisions of this legislation would have meant that those South Asian men who had married under Muslim or Hindu law that allowed polygamy were not validly married, even if the marriages were monogamous.

The Court of Appeal (in Hussain v Hussain [1982] 1 All ER 369) stepped in to partly remedy this anomaly by holding that since no English domiciled men were capable in law of entering into polygamous marriages, all such marriages were valid. However, the effect of the legislation and this case was still that those women married to men who were already married could have their marriages treated as invalid under English law if their husband was considered as domiciled in England.

However, children of such marriages were still considered legitimate under the Legitimacy Act 1976 and thus able to inherit British citizen status from their fathers (Pearl 1986: 48-49). Or so it was thought! The recent decision of the Court of Appeal in Azad v ECO, Dhaka (10 May 2001, [2000] WL 1918688 (CA), [2001] INLR 109, [2001] Imm AR 318) now puts the whole thing in doubt.

The applicant's child, born in Bangladesh in 1984, was a son by a third wife. An application was made for a certificate of entitlement to the right of abode in the UK on his behalf. It was also recognized that this would be a test case for all other children by the father's second and third wives.

By the Court of Appeal stage, some matters had already been conceded, specifically that the marriage between the applicant's father and mother was considered void under English law, even though valid under Bangladesh law, as the father was already domiciled 'in the United Kingdom'. The father, it was conceded, knew that to be so, and so it was the mother's belief as to validity on which the case would turn.

This is because s. 1 of the Legitimacy Act 1976 (as amended) provides in the relevant part as follows:

The child of a void marriage, whenever born, shall be treated as the legitimate child of his parents if, at the time of the insemination resulting in the birth or, where there was no such insemination, the child's conception (or at the time of the celebration of the marriage if later) both or either of the parties reasonably believed that the marriage was valid.

It is hereby declared for the avoidance of doubt that subsection above applies notwithstanding that the belief that the marriage was valid was due to a mistake as to the law.' As the Court saw it, the main question was whether the mother's belief was one as to validity under English law or under the lex loci celebrations, that is, Bangladesh law.

In an extremely briefly reasoned speech Jacob J, with whom Laws and Kennedy LJJ fully agreed, held that the question ought to be whether she had a reasonable belief in the validity of the marriage under English law. Jacob J also felt that, as there was no evidence as to the mother's state of mind, no finding could be made as to her belief.

He dismissed the test in an earlier Tribunal case (Begum, 16 March 1990) in which Prof. Jackson had suggested that the Tribunal would be prepared 'to approach the matter on the basis that it would suffice if one parent had no reason to believe that the marriage would be invalid in English law'. Given that there was no material from the third wife as to her belief about the position under English law, the Tribunal's decision in the present case was upheld.

This is an extremely worrying judgment. For observers who are used to decisions on South Asian laws being largely driven by immigration concerns it probably does not come as much of a surprise. However, it means that decision-makers are now able to refuse citizenship to children of polygamous married parents based on a belief about validity under English law that was held by either spouse even though that marriage was considered legal in the place where this was performed and, crucially, under the personal laws of the parties concerned.

Further, the decision on citizenship rests on an initial finding of illegitimacy that would have thoroughly offensive overtones to a significant number of communities (not only Bangladeshis) now settled in Britain. Not only may it already be considered offensive enough that English law does not respect polygamous arrangements allowed under the laws of large sections of the world's population, but it may not go unnoticed that English law is so easily prepared to declare children of such unions illegitimate.

Even though recognized under other legal systems, it is certainly the case that such divorces are routinely being de-recognized by UK decision-makers who are supported in this by case law from the highest courts (Pearl and Menski 1998: 382-398, Jones and Welhengama 2000: 118-132, Mayss 2000). As seen in the Shamsun Nahar case (above), there are even cases where English law has trouble recognizing first marriages where no official element of registration is involved. The fact that most legal systems in the world are happy to continue recognizing such marriages does not seem to make a difference in English law, however. Rather, in the face of increasing social pluralism, English law seems again to retreat further into an ethnocentric posture.

Glossary of terms:

Angrezi shariat	British Muslim law, here interpreted as the living law among Muslims, so not confined to textual/doctrinal sources (Menski in Pearl and Minks 1998), ingreji shoriyot in Bangla/Sylheti
Bidesh	abroad, foreign country
Desh bidesh	a home abroad or a home from home (Bangla, from Gardner 1993)
Desh pardesh	a home abroad or a home from home (Panjabi, Urdu, Gujarati, Hindi, from Ballard 1994)
Desh	country/home
Kagzi	of paper (literally, Urdu), here meant to signify 'bureaucratic', as in 'kagzi raj'
Quamic	capacity of religious ideas and loyalties to act as a vehicle for ethnopolitical mobilization (Ballard 1996)
Rivaz	custom, rules of appropriate behaviour within a family or community context (Ballard n.d.), rewaj in Bangla/Sylheti
Shari'a	Muslim law (but here qualified to also indicate textual or doctrinal sources of this law)
Zina	illicit sex, jina in Bangla/Sylheti

CHAPTER 5 – MIGRATION IN THE UK

5.1 Bangladeshi Immigrants:

This chapter begins with a discussion on Bangladeshi Immigrants. It then concentrates on Bangladeshis in the UK. It traces the root history of the Bangladeshi immigrants to this country. The chapter also attempts to draw a socioeconomic profile of Immigration. It indicates how they are connected to Bangladesh.

5.2 Global Bangladeshi Immigration:

5.2.1 Number:

There is no information readily available on the number of Bangladeshi long-term emigrants. The population census data of Bangladesh does not include information on migration, internal or international. BMET, the repository of information on short-term migration, does not have any mechanism to keep a record of the long-term migrants.

This study has tried to collate information from informed sources having first-hand knowledge of the long-term immigrants of Bangladesh. The figures provided are mostly their estimation. The countries on which such estimation was available are UK, USA, Italy, Japan, Australia, Greece, Canada, Spain, Germany, South Africa, France, Netherlands, Belgium, and Switzerland.

5.2.2 Number of Bangladeshi immigrants in industrialised countries.

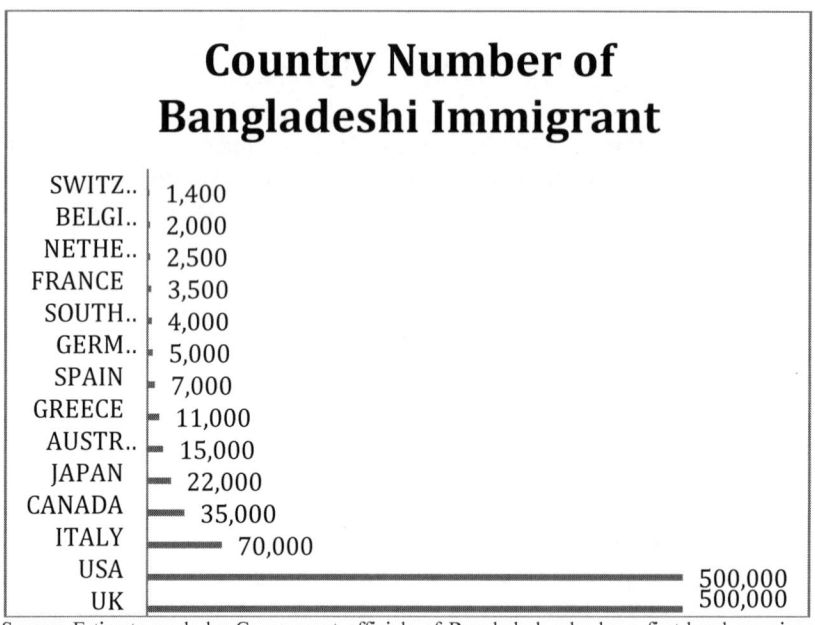

Country Number of Bangladeshi Immigrant

Country	Number
SWITZ..	1,400
BELGI..	2,000
NETHE..	2,500
FRANCE	3,500
SOUTH..	4,000
GERM..	5,000
SPAIN	7,000
GREECE	11,000
AUSTR..	15,000
JAPAN	22,000
CANADA	35,000
ITALY	70,000
USA	500,000
UK	500,000

Source: Estimate made by Government officials of Bangladesh who have first-hand experience with the immigrant community.

This table presents the estimated number of Bangladeshi immigrants in those countries. It provides estimates of fourteen countries. In these countries, there are about 1.178 million Bangladeshis who are now living abroad permanently either as a citizen or with other valid documents.

The population census data of the UK put the figure of Bangladeshis immigrants around 447,201. However, the ethnic Bangladeshi press and those who have information, claim that there are 500,000 Bangladeshis in the UK.

5.3 Bangladeshi Immigrants in the UK:

In this section, detailed research is made on the UK concerning the basis of available secondary information. Quite a few studies have been undertaken with regards to migration of Bangladeshis in the UK, (Eade, Vemplew & Peach (1990), Wrench & Qureshi (1996), Gardner (1995), Samad & Eade (2002), and Carey & Shukur (1985). Ahmed Kaufman & Naim (1996), Haddad (1986), Ali (1996).

5.3.1 History of Immigration:

Migration history of people from the area that now constitutes Bangladesh has been quite long in the making. Tracing mythology, Sri Lankans believe that Singhala communities first migrated to Sri Lanka from this area. Aatish Dipangkar, the Buddhist scholar-traveler carried the knowledge of earthen embankment cross-dam to China during the 10th century. During the British period, people from this area also migrated to Assam and Burma.

However, the migration on an organised scale in the UK of course was intimately connected to that of British colonialism. Bangladeshis gained the reputation as 'Lashkar' or seamen over the late nineteenth century and early twentieth century. In the Bangladeshi context seamen mostly originated from the southeast part of the country, i.e., Chittagong and Noakhali, which face the Bay of Bengal. People from those areas found jobs in British ships, which carried goods from Calcutta (India) all over the world. People from the Sylhet region that was not adjoining the sea also joined the British merchant navy as 'Khalashis', cooks, cook-mates, and cleaners.

Experts on Sylheti migration speculate that this group did not have much experience with the sea and they jumped ship at the first opportunity. Due to the 'ship jumping' tendency of the seamen, a small settlement of the Bangladeshis, especially Sylheti persons have been established in port. Those who jumped ship in the UK ended up settling in London, Liverpool, and Bristol.

Concept Paper on Building Capacity of Ministry of Expatriates' Welfare and Overseas Employment, IOM, Dhaka, 2002 also made a similar rough estimation. According to this estimate, the number of long-term EBs is 1.05 million. Section of them may have joined the British merchant ships (Alam, 1988)

5.3.2 Pioneer migrants of Bangladeshis:

The pioneer migrants of Bangladeshis' who landed in the UK were predominantly of Sylheti origin. The early migrants in the UK found jobs as labourers in different industries. Early migrants in the UK were mostly illiterate. They represented landless peasantry and all of them were male. In the case of the UK, some of the early settlers got married to the locals and established their families in the host country.

The second wave of migration to the UK started in the 1950s. The British Government adopted a policy to encourage labour migration from its erstwhile colonies, as there was an acute labour shortage after World War II. Once the British Government introduced its new immigration policy, a section of the sea-faring migrants who had by then settled in the UK, sponsored their families from their villages and towns.

Arriving as young men in the post-war period most lived and worked in the northern cities such as Birmingham, Bradford, Leeds, Sheffield, Rochdale, Tameside, Manchester, and Oldham. They found employment in heavy industries. Some went to London, worked in the garment trade as pressers or tailors. During the 1970s, the heavy industry sector of the UK was declining and a large number of Bangladeshis lost their jobs.

This brought many Sylhetis to London from the northwest of the UK. In the 1980s they started bringing their wives and children to the UK on a large scale. A small number of highly educated people representing the upper and middle class of Bangladeshi urban society also migrated to Europe even before the Second World War. They came to the UK for higher education. Gradually they entered professional life in the UK and changed their legal status into citizens. Nonetheless, the number of those who came as non-economic migrants is relatively small.

5.3.3 Number of Bangladeshi Immigrants in the UK:

The exact number of Bangladeshi Immigrants living in the UK will always be difficult to arrive at because of the reasons mentioned below. The table shown in the next point shows that up to 1961, the total Bangladeshi population originating from East Pakistan in the UK which was 6,000. In the next thirty years, it rose to 162,835. Amongst them, 105,012 were Bangladesh born and 59,679 were born in the UK. According to the most recent 2011 census the total Bangladeshi population is 447,201.

Peach (1990) suggests that the number of Bangladeshi children born in Britain doubled from 16,000 to 32,000 between 1981 and 1985/87 and doubled again between 1985/87 and 1991 census. In 1991, 36.4% of the Bangladeshi population was born in the UK. The 2001 Census shows that the total number of Bangladeshi Immigrants in the UK had risen to 300,000 and according to the 2011 Census total Bangladeshi population is 447,201 amongst them Bangladeshi-born children 142,319. However, the ethnic Bangladeshi media holds that the current number of Bangladeshi immigrants should be around 500,000.

5.3.4 Estimate of growth of Bangladeshi population in UK 1961-2011

Year	Bangladeshi born	UK born Bangladeshis	Total ethnic BD population
1961	6,000	-	6,000
1971	21,000	1,000	22,000
1981	48,517	16,000	64,561
1985/87	79,000	32,000	111,000
1991	105,012	59,679	162,835
2001	124,355	283,065	162,835
2011	142,319	-	447,201

Source: Data of 1961, 71, 81 censuses, is gathered from Peach (1990), 1985/87 data is from 'Labour Force Survey' and 2011 census of UK. The data source of 2001 is weekly Patrika, October 2002.

5.4. Geographical Coverage:

The Bangladeshi population in the UK is overwhelmingly located in England (97%). Again, in England, the bulk of the Bangladeshi population live in the largest urban centres of Greater London, the West Midlands, and Greater Manchester. Nearly half of the London Bangladeshis are found in the single Borough of Tower Hamlets, which hosts a quarter of the total Bangladeshis living in the UK. (Source: 1991 census). Tower Hamlets and the neighbouring London Boroughs of Newham, Hackney, Haringey, Islington, and Camden together contained 37% of the Bangladeshi population of Great Britain in 1991. (Wrench & Qureshi, 1996).

According to the census of 2011, 222,127 Bangladeshis are residing in London, making up just fewer than 2% of the total city population. The numbers are projected to increase by over a third by 2011 (Kenny, 2002). The next largest concentration is in Birmingham.

5.4.1 Socio-Economic Profile:

Male-Female Ration:
There are more men than women amongst the immigrants in the UK. According to the 1991 census in the UK, males outnumbered females in the Bangladeshi ethnic group, with 1091 males for every 1000 females (Wrench & Qureshi 1996). It also shows that the male-female ratio of British-born Bangladeshis is more or less symmetrical. Therefore, the gender imbalance is a

feature of those who were born in Bangladesh. The male dominance is particularly marked in the 50 years and older age group. The average age of Bangladeshi husbands is 5 years more than Bangladeshi wives.

Age:
In the UK, Bangladeshis are one of the youngest population groups. In 2001, amongst the Bangladeshi Immigrants in the UK, nearly twice as many are under the age of 15 than the Caucasian ethnic population (33% compared with 17%). Just over 5% of the Bangladeshi Immigrant in the UK is aged 60 and over, whereas 19% of the Caucasian ethnic population belongs to that age group. According to the 2011 Census, the North West Bangladeshi population is 45,897.

Education:
In the UK, it is well known that during the 1950s and 1960s, when major migration flow took place, men from rural Sylhet with very little educational background joined the UK labor force to work in local factories. This less educated status is reflected in the educational status of the whole Bangladeshi Immigrants in the UK. Two-fifths of the Bangladeshi working-age population in the UK does not possess any educational qualifications (Kenny, 2002).

The UK-born Bangladeshi population is enrolled in schools. In 1999, 30% of the young Bangladeshi Immigrants achieved 5 or more grades between A and C in General School Certificate Examinations. This is, however, less than the Indian ethnic community in the UK and the Caucasian ethnic community. 62% of the young expatriates of Indian origin have been able to reach such grades and in the case of the Caucasian ethnic population, 50% reached that.

In the last few years, a small number of youths have been prepared to stay at schools, or go into higher education to study electronics, engineering, law, teachers' training, and youth and community work. (Carey & Shukur 1985)

Marital status:
In the UK, according to the 1991 census, the percentages of Bangladeshi men and women married and single were similar to those of white ethnic groups, except that a rather higher percentage of Bangladeshi women were married. Bangladeshi people were less likely to be widowed or divorced. Divorce was much less common among Bangladeshi Immigrants than the Caucasian ethnic population.

Occupation:
In the UK nearly two-thirds of the Bangladeshi men aged sixteen and over are in manual employment. 16% of them are in professional and managerial positions. Bangladeshis were the latest immigrants to revive the garment industry and to create ethnic enclaves of small shops, cafes, restaurants, taxi companies, and travel agencies. The industrial distribution of work for Bangladeshi men is very different.

More than two-thirds work in the distribution sector covering retailing, restaurants, and other catering services with the largest other sources of employment being textiles and clothing, health, and education. (Wrench & Qureshi 1996).

The second and third generations of Bangladeshis are eager to find work outside the ethnic niche. A good number of Bangladeshis are now in business, restaurants being the major growth industry where the Bangladeshi Immigrants are doing extremely well. Bangladeshi women are predominantly working in other skilled trades, clerical occupations, and personal services, sales, and teaching. A higher percentage of Bangladeshi women are working in unskilled jobs (Wrench & Qureshi: 1996).

5.4.2 Labour Force Participation and Unemployment:

In 1991, 74.3% of the male Bangladeshi Immigrant in the UK was participating in the labour force. In the UK, compared to other ethnic groups Bangladeshis suffer higher rates of unemployment. In the 1991 census, 22.7% of British-Bangladeshi males of 16 years and above were unemployed with the national average of 12.6%. (Samad and Eade: 2002. This is the highest among the black and other minority groups (Kenny: 2002).

Women's participation in the labour market is very low. Only 22.2% of the Bangladeshi women aged 16 and over are economically active compared to the national average of 50% (Eade, Vamplew, Peach 1996).

Income:
Bangladeshi Immigrants have the lowest ever earnings of all ethnic groups. In 2000-01, Bangladeshi workers earned an average of £5.92 per hour compared with £12.11 for employees from Caucasian ethnic groups and 25% of the Bangladeshi women earned less than £3.75 per hour.

5.4.3 Remittance Flow:

From the discussion above it is clear that the socio-economic condition of Bangladeshi Immigrants of the UK is not homogenous. A section of them is quite well off, whereas some other sections may not be in good economic condition. Macro-level data also reveals that those belonging to the professional category are relatively small, whereas a large section of the Bangladeshi Immigrants is associated with small services. Some represent very high educational qualifications, while others are less educated, or uneducated.

An important trait of this group is their propensity to remit money home for some reason or the other. Table 5.4.5 the country-wise and year-wise remittances sent to Bangladesh from 1997 to November 2002. One can see from the table, The UK is an important remittance-sending country. During the 1950s and 1960s, these were the two major remittance-sending countries for Bangladesh.

5.4.4 Year-wise growth of remittance flow from the UK (In million pounds)

From 1997-2002.

Year	Amount	%Increase
1997	59.43	--
1998	62.95	5.92
1999	54.85	-12.86
2000	68.87	25.56
2001	63.93	-7.17
2002(Nov.)	151.43	136.86
1997-2002	461.46	29.66

Source: prepared based on BMET data of 2003.

5.4.5 Year-wise remittance flow of wage earners to Bangladesh from Jan '97 to Nov '02.

5.5 CONCLUSION

This chapter provided a cursory idea about global Bangladeshi Immigrants. It was seen that there is a Bangladeshi Immigrants population within the region. However, this is assimilated into their country of residence. Moreover, the historical context within the region has its uniqueness. The chapter also establishes that there are a good number of long-term emigrants dispersed around the world but there hardly exists any data about their number.

This chapter also attempted to trace the processes of migration and settlement of Bangladeshis in the UK. Pioneer migrants were the 'ship jumpers'. However, the migration pattern changed significantly during the 1960s. In that decade, skilled and professionals mainly got the opportunity to migrate to the US, whereas in the UK it is the families of first-generation migrants from the same kind of rural socio-economic background who migrated to the UK to work as a labourer in the heavy industries. By the 1970s, such migration again got restricted in the UK and family reunification remained as the only major avenue for migration.

CHAPTER 6 - British Bangladeshi

A British Bangladeshi (Bengali) is a person of Bangladeshi origin who resides in the United Kingdom having emigrated to the UK and attained citizenship through naturalisation or whose parents did so; they are also known as British Bangladeshis. Large numbers of Bangladeshis immigrated to the UK, primarily from Sylhet, located in the northeast of the country, mainly during the 1960's and 1970s.

The largest concentration of Bangladeshi people is in London, primarily in the east London boroughs, of which Tower Hamlets has the highest proportion, making up approximately 37% of the borough's total population. This large diaspora in London leads people in Bangladesh to refer to British Bangladeshis as "Londonis". Bangladeshis also have significant communities in Luton, Birmingham, Hyde, Oldham, Rochdale, Manchester, Bradford, Leeds, Newcastle upon Tyne, Cardiff, and Sunderland.

Bangladeshis form one of the UK's largest immigrant groups and are also one of its youngest and fastest-growing communities. The population of Bangladeshis in Britain has grown steadily over the years. At the time of the 2001 UK Census, 154,362 Bangladeshi-born people were residents in the UK, and there were a total of 283,063 residents of Bangladeshi ethnicity.

According to the 2011 Census total Bangladeshi population is 447,201 amongst them Bangladeshi-born children 142,319.

By 2007, the ethnic Bangladeshi population in England was only estimated to be 353,900. Estimates suggest about 500,000 Bangladeshis are residing in the UK. According to the 2011 Census, the total Bangladeshi population is 447,201. Bangladeshis from a largely homogeneous community. Rates of unemployment are typically high; there is overcrowding and some health problems.

The latest generation of Bangladeshis, however, form a thriving community that is beginning to establish itself in the mainstream of commerce and politics. Despite being the most recently settled of the major South Asian communities in Britain, the Bangladeshis are well established throughout the communities.

6.1 History of Bangladeshis in the United Kingdom:

Bengalis had been present in Britain as early as the 19th century. The records of first arrivals from the region what is known today as Bangladesh (was British India), were Sylhet cooks in London during 1873, part of the East India Company, who arrived in the UK as lascars in ships to work in restaurants.author Caroline Adams records that in 1925 a lost Bengali man was searching for other Bengali settlers in London.

These first few arrivals started the process of "chain migration" mainly from one region of Bangladesh—Sylhet, which led to substantial numbers of people migrating from rural areas of the region, creating links between relatives in Britain and the region.They mainly immigrated to the United Kingdom to find work, achieve a better living standard, and escape the conflict.

During the pre-state years, the 1950s and 1960s, Bengali men immigrated to London in search of employment.

In 1971 Bangladesh, (known until then as "East Pakistan"), fought for its independence from Pakistan in what was known as the Bangladesh Liberation War. In the region of Sylhet, this led some people to join the Mukti Bahini or Liberation Army.However, the war also caused large numbers of Sylhet people to flee, mainly to Britain.

In the 1970s, changes in immigration laws encouraged a new wave of Bangladeshis to come to the UK and settle. Job opportunities were initially limited to low-paid sectors, with unskilled-semi-skilled work in small factories and the textile trade being common. When the "Indian' restaurant" concept became popular, some Sylhetis started to open cafes. From these small beginnings, a network of Bangladeshi restaurants, shops, and other small businesses became established in these areas. The influence of Bangladeshi culture and diversity began to develop across the East London boroughs.

The early immigrants lived in overcrowded accommodation. The men were often illiterate, poorly educated, and spoke little English, so could not interact well with the English-speaking population and could not enter higher education.Some became targets for English businessmen, who sold their properties to other Sylhetis, even though they had no legal claims to the buildings.

By the late 1970s, the Brick Lane area had become predominantly Bengali, replacing the former Jewish community which had declined. Following the increase in the number of Bengalis in the area, the Jews migrated to the outlying suburbs of London, as they integrated with the majority British population. Jewish bakeries were turned into curry houses, jewellery shops became sari stores, and synagogues became dress factories.

The synagogue at the corner of Fournier Street and Brick Lane became the Jammeh Masjid or the 'Great London Mosque', which continues to serve the Bangladeshi community to this day.This building represents the history of successive communities of immigrants in this part of London. It was built in 1743 as a French Protestant church; in 1819 it became a Methodist chapel, and in 1898 was designated as the Spitalfields Great Synagogue. It was finally sold, to become the Jammeh Masjid.

The period also however saw a rise in the number of attacks on Bangladeshis in the area, in a reprise of the racial tension of the 1930s, when Oswald Mosley's Black shirts had marched against the Jewish communities. In nearby Bethnal Green, the anti-immigrant National Front became active, distributing leaflets on the streets and holding meetings. White youths were known as "skinheads" who appeared in the Brick Lane area, vandalising property and reportedly spitting at Bengali children and assaulting women. Bengali children were allowed out of school early; women walked to work in groups to shield them from potential violence. Parents began to impose curfews on their children, for their safety; flats were protected against racially motivated arson by the installation of fire-proof letterboxes.

Protest March by Bangladeshis to Downing Street with murdered Altab Ali's coffin, 1978

On 4 May 1978, Altab Ali, a 25-year-old Bangladeshi clothing worker, was murdered by three teenage boys as he walked home from work, in a racially motivated attack. The murder took place near the corner of Adler Street and Whitechapel Road, by St Mary's Churchyard. This murder mobilized the Bangladeshi community.

Demonstrations were held in Brick Lane against the National Front and groups such as the Bangladesh Youth Movement was formed. On 14th May over 7,000 people, mostly Bangladeshis took part in a demonstration against racial violence, marching behind Altab Ali's coffin to Hyde Park. Some youths formed local gangs and carried out reprisal attacks on their skinhead opponents.

The name Altab Ali became associated with a movement of resistance against racist attacks and remains linked with this struggle for human rights. His murder was the trigger for the first significant political organisation against racism by local Bangladeshis. Today's identification and association of British Bangladeshis with Tower Hamlets owes much to this campaign.

A park has been named after Altab Ali, at the street where he was murdered.In 1993 racial violence was incited by the anti-immigration British National Party (BNP); several Bangladeshi students were severely injured, but the BNP's attempted inroads were stopped after demonstrations of Bangladeshi resolve.

In 1988, a "friendship link" between the city of St Albans in Hertfordshire and the region of Sylhet was created by the district council. This link between the two cities was established when the council supported housing projects in the city as part of the International Year of Shelter for the Homeless initiative. It was also created because Sylhet is the area of origin for the largest ethnic minority group in St Albans.In April 2001, the London Borough of Tower Hamlets council officially renamed the 'Spitalfields' electoral ward Spitalfields and Banglatown. Surrounding streets were redecorated, with lamp posts painted in green and red, the colours of the Bangladeshi flag.By this stage, the majority living in the ward were of Bangladeshi origin—nearly 60% of the population.

6.2 Population:

British Bangladeshis are people who have emigrated from Bangladesh to the United Kingdom. They have mainly settled in the boroughs of East London, primarily in the borough of Tower Hamlets, Camden, Haringey, Hackney, Newham, Westminster, and Redbridge. Over 50% of the Bangladeshi population living in the United Kingdom live in London.

Census Population

Year	Population	+/- & %
1961	6,000	-
1971	22,000	+266.7%
1981	64,561	+193.5%
1991	162,835	+152.2%
2001	283,063	+73.8%
2011	447,201	

Bangladeshis in the UK are largely a youthful population, heavily concentrated in London's inner boroughs. According to the 2011 Census 447,201 Bangladeshis lived in the United Kingdom, forming 0.8% of the total population.Based on the latest statistics by the Office for National Statistics, there were 447, 201 Bangladeshis living in England and Wales as of 2011, it is however estimated that there are around 500,000 Bangladeshis in the UK.
London's Bangladeshi population was 153,893, representing 54.37% of the UK Bangladeshi population (2001). The highest concentrations were found

in Tower Hamlets, where Bangladeshis constituted 33.5% of the borough population (22.8% of the UK Bangladeshi population) and in Newham, accounting for 9% of the borough population.

According to the recent 2011 census, the London Bangladeshi population is 222,127 (highest in the UK), the second-largest Bangladeshi population is in the West Midland (52,477) and thirdly in the Northwest (45,897). There are 6,437 Bangladeshis in Manchester, 4,296 Bangladeshis in Tameside, 16,310 Bangladeshis in Oldham, 4,342 Bangladeshis in Rochdale, 605 Bangladeshis in Salford.

More than half of the United Kingdom's Bangladeshis—approximately 53%—were born in Bangladesh.Bangladesh ranks third in the list of countries of birth for Londoners born outside the United Kingdom.Bangladeshis are one of the youngest of the UK's ethnic populations; 38% under the age of 16, 59% are aged 16–64, and only 3% are aged 65 and over. The census also revealed a heavy predominance in the male population, which was 64% of the total.

6.3 Bangladeshi communities in different towns and cities:

All the data below is based on the 2011 Census is for Bangladeshi people in England and Wales regardless of birthplace (excluding those of partial Bangladeshi origin).

Area.	Population of Bangladeshis.
Northeast	10,972
Northwest	45,897
Southeast	27,951
Southwest	8,416
East Midlands	13,258
West Midlands	52,477
East of England	32,992
London	222,127
Wales	10,687
Yorkshire and the Humber	22,424

Greater Manchester.	Population Of Bangladeshis.
Bolton	614
Bury	311
Manchester	6,437
Oldham	16,310
Rochdale	4,342
Salford	605
Stockport	705
Tameside	4,296
Trafford	457
Wigan	109

6.4 Employment and Education:

Bangladeshis are now mainly employed in the distribution, hotels, and restaurant industries.In 2001 and 2002, Bangladeshis had the highest unemployment rate in Britain, at 20% for men and 24% for women; over 40% of Bangladeshi men younger than 25 years old were unemployed. In Tower Hamlets 32% of people aged between 18–25 years old were unemployed. The average earnings of the Bangladeshis were £150 per week.

New generation Bangladeshis, however, aspire to professional careers, becoming doctors, IT management specialists, and teachers, and in business.In education, Bangladeshi pupils have registered below the average national academic achievement levels, but these results have steadily improved, particularly amongst Bangladeshi girls; this applies both to Key stage levels and GCSEs.

Ofsted reports from secondary schools have shown that many Bangladeshi pupils are making significant progress, compared with other ethnic minority groups.Girls are more likely to do better in education than boys; 55% of girls are achieving 5 or more A*-C at GCSE, compared to 41% boys. The overall achievement rate for Bangladeshi pupils is 48%, compared with 53% for all UK pupils.

6.5 Health and Housing:

Bangladeshis had the highest rates of illness in the UK, in 2001. Bangladeshi men were three times as likely to visit their doctor as men in the general population. Bangladeshis also had the highest rates of people with disabilities and were more likely to smoke than any other ethnic group, at a rate of 44% in

1999 in England. Smoking was very common amongst the men, but very few women smoked, perhaps due to cultural customs.

The average number of people living in each Bangladeshi household is 4.8,larger than all other ethnic groups. Households which contained a single person were 9%; houses containing a married couple were 54%, pensioner households were 2%. Bangladeshis living in London were 40 times more likely to be living in cramped and poor housing types of housing than anyone else in the country. There were twice as many people per room as Caucasian households, with 43% living in homes with insufficient bedroom space.

For these reasons, many are moving out of Tower Hamlets to larger housing estates.A third of Bangladeshi homes contain more than one family—64% of all overcrowded households in Tower Hamlets are Bangladeshi.In England and Wales, only 37% of Bangladeshis owned households compared to 69% of the population, those with social rented tenure is 48%, the largest of which in Tower Hamlets (82%) and Camden (81%).

6.6 Origins:

British Bangladeshis predominantly originate from the north-eastern region of Sylhet (95%).Many families originate from different Upazilas or thanas across Sylhet, which includes the districts of Sylhet, Sunamganj, Habiganj, and Maulvibazar. The largest places of origin are in the Upazilas of, Jagannathpur, Beanibazar, and Biswanath.

Other places within the Sylhet region which also have large numbers of expatriates include, Moulvibazar, Golapganj, Nabiganj, and many others across the region.The minorities from outside Sylhet are mainly from Noakhali, Chittagong, and Khulna, very few are from other divisions. The majority of Bangladeshis speak Sylheti.The language is sometimes considered as a dialect of Bengali and does not have a written form.

Although many Sylheti speakers say they speak Bengali, this is because they do not expect outsiders to be well informed about dialects.Bengali/Sylheti is the second largest language spoken after English in London.97% of Bangladeshi students speak English as a second language, after Sylheti.In recent years, there has been a slight increase in the numbers of Bangladeshi students arriving in the United Kingdom; the majority of these are from Dhaka and other regions. Many of these are on student Visas, living in the East London areas amongst the Bangladeshi communities.

6.7 Culture:

The majority of British Bengalis regard Bangladesh as their "ancestral home"; although a survey showed strong feelings that they belonged to the British society.The cultural traditions practiced in Bangladesh are also widely practiced by the community. The languages of Sylheti and Bengali are viewed as important features of cultural identity; parents, therefore, encourage young people to attend standard Bengali classes to learn the language,although many find this learning progress difficult in the UK.English tends to be spoken amongst younger brothers and sisters and groups and Bengali/Sylheti with parents. Communities share and favour a family-orientated community culture.

6.8 Celebrations:

Crowds at the Baishakhi Mela in London:

Significant Bengali events or celebrations are celebrated by the community annually. The Baishakhi Mela is a celebration of the Bengali New Year, celebrated by the Bangladeshi community every year. Held each April–May since 1997 in London's Banglatown, it is the largest Asian open-air event in Europe and the largest Bengali festival outside Bangladesh. In Bangladesh and West Bengal, it is known as the Pohela Boishakh.

The event is broadcast live across different continents; it features a funfair, music, and dance displays on stages, with people dressed in colourful traditional clothes, in Weavers Field and Allen Gardens in Bethnal Green.The Mela is also designed to enhance the area's community identity, bringing together the best of Bengali culture.

Brick Lane is the main destination where curry and Bengali spices are served throughout the day. As of 2009, the Mela was organised by the Tower Hamlets council, attracting 95,000 people, featuring popular artists such as Momtaz Begum, Nukul Kumar Bishwash, Mumzy, and many others.

6.8.1 The Language Movement Day (Shaheed Dibosh):

The Language Movement Day commemorates the martyrdom of the people killed in the demonstrations of 1952 for the Bengali language; the arch incorporates a complex Bengali-style pattern, meant to show the merging of different cultures in East London.A similar monument was built in Westwood, in Oldham, through a local council regeneration.This event is taken place at midnight on 20th February, where the Bengali community comes together to lay wreaths at the monument.

In the London borough of Tower Hamlets, the Shaheed Minar was designated in Altab Ali Park in 1999. At the entrance to the park is an arch created by David Peterson, developed as a memorial to Altab Ali and other victims of the racist attacks.

6.9 Marriage

Same cultural rituals are practiced

Bangladeshi weddings are celebrated with a combination of Bengali and Muslim traditions and play a large part in developing and maintaining social ties. Many marriages of Bangladeshis are between the British (Londonis) and Bangladeshi-born; sometimes men will go to Bangladesh to get married, however, over the years more women are marrying in Bangladesh.

Marriages between relatives are common and increase relationships within extended families. Second or third-generation Bangladeshis are more likely to get married in the UK, within the British culture, exposure to which has created a division between preferences for arranged marriages or love marriages.under the traditional practice, the bride's family must buy the groom's family a whole new set of furniture, which is housed in the family home, all original furniture is either thrown out or given away.

The average Bangladeshi community will spend from £30-60,000 for a single wedding within the community, which includes the decorations, the venue, food, clothing, and limousines, all areas in which there is competition between families.Forced marriages are rare, however, the practice is largely present in Bangladesh, and the British High Commission has been involved with many cases concerning British citizens.

These include Nasrin Begum, a 19-year-old teenager who travelled from the UK to Bangladesh with her mother in 2008,she contacted the British consular office in Sylhet to intervene and was rescued by embassy officials in the village.Another media highlight includes a Bangladeshi-born National Health Service doctor Humaira Abedin, she was deceived by her parents after asking her to arrive at their home in Dhaka,a court-ordered her parents to hand her over to the British High Commission.The commission has been reported to have handled 56 cases from April 2007 to March 2008.

6.10 Media

There are five Bengali channels available on satellite television in Britain. Two British-owned channels are Channel S,and Bangla TV.There are popular national channels, ATN Bangla, NTV, Channel i and Channel 9 are also available.

Bengali newspapers have been increasing within the community, such include Surma News Group. The East End Life (local newspaper of the borough) also includes a section for Bengali readers.The first international film is based on a story about British Bangladeshis in the Brick Lane (2007), based on the novel by author Monica Ali, her book is about a woman who moves to London from rural Bangladesh, with her husband, wedded in an arranged marriage.

The film was critically acclaimed, and the novel was an award-winning bestseller. The film however caused some controversy within the community.Other films created in the community are mainly based on the struggles which British Bangladeshis face such as drugs and presenting a culture clash. These dramas include Shopner Desh (2006) - a story related to culture clashes.

6.11 Religion:

The East London Mosque & London Muslim Centre located in Whitechapel, London
The Bangladeshi population is dominated by one religion, Islam. Out of all the ethnic groups in the UK, it has the largest proportion of people following a single religion. Nearly all Bangladeshis are Sunni Muslims;the 2001 census in

England and Wales showed those who indicated their religion, 92.5% were Muslim, and 1.2% follow other religions (mostly Hindu and Christian).

In London, Bangladeshi Muslims make up 24% of all London Muslims, more than any other single ethnic group in the capital.The largest affiliations are the Deobandi movement (mainly of Tablighi Jamaat),the Jamaat-e-Islami movement, andthe Sufi Barelvi (includes
the Fultali movement).The Hizb ut-Tahrir and the Salafi movement also have a small following.

Most Bangladeshis regard themselves as part of the ummah, basing their identity on their religion rather than their ethnic group. A majority of older women wear the burqa, and many young women are opting to wear a hijab, a traditional women's headscarf—whereas, in Bangladesh, comparatively very few women do so; this has been described as a "British phenomenon".

Arabic is also learned by children, many of whom attend Qur'an classes at mosques or the madrasah.Many male youths are also involved with Islamic groups,which include the Young Muslim Organisation, affiliated with the Islamic Forum Europe. This group is based in Tower Hamlets and has thus attracted mainly young Bangladeshi Muslims. It has been increasingly associated with the East London Mosque, which is one of the largest mosques used predominantly by Bangladeshis.In 2004, the mosque created a new extension attached, the London Muslim Centre which holds up to 10,000 people.

6.12 Festivals:

Religious Muslim festivals are celebrated by the community each year, which includes Eid al-Adha and Eid-ul-Fitr. People are dressed in their new traditional clothing such as sherwani or salwar kameez.Children are given money by elders, and Eid prayers are attended by men in the morning in large numbers, they will then visit their relatives later in the day. Traditional food will be cooked for relatives, such as samosa or Sandesh.

The celebration of Eid reunites relatives and improves relations.In the evening, young people will spend the remaining time socialising with friends. Some, however, will go "cruising" – traveling across cities in expensive hired cars, playing loud music, and sometimes waving the Bangladesh flag. Sociologists suggest these British Bangladeshi boys and girls have reinterpreted the older, more traditional practice of their faith and culture.

The Eid-al-Adha is celebrated after Eid-ul-Fitr, to commemorate the prophet Ibrahim's compliance to sacrifice his son Isma'il. An animal has to be sacrificed, and then distributed between families and neighbours as Zakat, however sometimes in the UK this is not practiced and the meat is purchased, therefore there is much difficulty for expatriates to celebrate the event. Some instead of distributing meat pay Zakat to mosques or others however send large sums of money to families in Bangladesh, for the purchase of cows.

6.13 Bangladeshi Society:

Bangladesh did not exist as a distinct geographic and ethnic unity until independence. The region had been a part of successive Indian empires, and during the British period, it formed the eastern part of a hinterland of Bengal, which was dominated by the British rulers and Hindu professional, commercial, and landed elites.

After the establishment of Pakistan in 1947, present-day Bangladesh came under the hegemony of the non-Bengali Muslim elites of the West Wing of Pakistan. The establishment of Bangladesh, therefore, implied the formation of both a new nation and a new social order.

6.13.1 Contribution:

They became politically active, mainly at the local level, although some achieved national prominence. Rushanara Ali is the first person of Bangladeshi origin to have been elected as a member of parliament during the 2010 general election for the Labour Party from the constituency of Bethnal Green and Bow, winning by a large majority of more than 10,000.

Baroness Uddin was the first Bangladeshi and Muslim woman to enter the House of Lords; she swore the oath of office in her faith

Anwar Choudhury became the British High Commissioner for Bangladesh in 2004, the first non-white British person to be appointed in a senior diplomatic post.

Lutfur Rahman is the first directly elected mayor of Tower Hamlets.

Rushanara Ali MP is he first elected Bangladeshi/Sylheti Female MP in Tower Hamlets and Britain.

Dr. Muhammad Abdul Bari is the chairman of the Muslim Council of Britain - the largest Muslim organisation in Britain.

Murad Qureshi, a Labour politician, is a member of the Greater London Assembly.

Others have contributed to the British media and business worlds.

Konica Haque is the longest-serving female presenter in Blue Peter, a BBC television programme for children

National TV presenters have included Lisa Aziz of Sky News,

Nina Hossain (ITV and BBC London)

Tasmin Lucia Khan (BBC News).

In drama, Shefali Chowdhury starred in the Harry Potter movies as Parvati Patil

Afshan Noor Azad-Kazi starred in the Harry Potter movies as Padma Patil

Mumzy is an R&B and hip-hop music artist, the first Bangladeshi to be releasing a music single.

Syed Ahmed is a businessman and also a television star, well known for being a candidate on The Apprentice.

There are many other entrepreneurs.

including the late Abdul Latif, known for his dish "Curry Hell";

Iqbal Ahmed, placed at number 511 on the Sunday Times Rich List 2006

Celebrity chef Tommy Miah

Rizwan Hussain is also very well known for TV presenting Islamic and charity shows on Channel S and Islam Channel, mainly known within the community.

Artists include Akram Khan, dancer, and choreographer

Runa Islam, a visual artist on film and photography

In Sport, the only Bangladeshi professional footballer in England is Anwar Uddin.

Writers which have received praise and criticism for their books include Ed Husain, who wrote the book The Islamist on account of his experience for five years with the Hizb ut-Tahrir, Monica Ali for her book Brick Lane a story based on a Bangladeshi woman, and Kia Abdullah for her book, Life, Love and Assimilation.

Large numbers of people from the Bangladeshi community have also been involved with local government, increasingly in the London borough of Tower Hamlets, and Camden. The majority of the councillors in Tower Hamlets are of Bangladeshi descent and part of the Labour Party. As of 2009, 32 of the total 51 councillors were Bangladeshi (63%), 18 were White (35%), and Somali (2%).The first Bangladeshi mayor in the country was Ghulam Murtuza in Tower Hamlets, and Camden has appointed many Bangladeshis as mayors since the first, Nasim Ali.

6.13.2 Political identity

In Bangladeshi politics, there are two groups, favouring different principles, one Islamic and the other secular. Between these groups, there has always been rivalry; however, the Islamic faction is steadily growing. This division between religious and secular was an issue during the Bangladesh Liberation War; the political history of Bangladesh is now is being re-interpreted again, in the UK.

The secular group show nationalism through monuments, or the introduction of Bengali culture, and the Islamic group mainly through dawah.

109

One symbol of Bengali nationalism is the Shaheed Minar replica, which commemorates the Bengali Language Movement, present in Oldham, as of today - the park is also the main venue for rallies and demonstrations, and in Westwood, Oldham.The monuments are a smaller replica of the one in Dhaka, Bangladesh, and symbolizes a mother and the martyred sons.Nationalism is mainly witnessed during celebrations of the mela, when groups such as the Swadhinata Trust try to promote Bengali history and heritage amongst young people, in schools, youth clubs, and community centres.

Islamic activists stress the commitment to a religious type of identity. These groups expanded their role in the local community by creating youth groups, providing lectures on Islam, and influencing people to be more involved with community mosques. These groups also describe Bengali secular nationalism as a "waste of money", a way to abstract from being Islamic: they claim to believe that the Baishakhi Mela celebrations are "shirk" activities.

Tension has arisen between the groups, with Islamists and nationalists being criticized or attacked.These incidents illustrate the competition for social and political control between Islamists and secularists in the community context. This sphere is highly dependent on collective memory and historical reinterpretations of the Liberation War.

6.14 Business:

Bangladeshi-owned Indian restaurants on Brick Lane

British-Bangladeshisare people who arrived from Bangladesh to the United Kingdom, and throughout the years have started to create new Restaurant businesses throughout the country. Bangladeshis were the first to have started the Curry Industry in the UK, from small businesses. The curry is now regarded as Britain's favourite dish. Many others also own supermarket stores specialising in Bangladeshi products, and also in the media, Bengali TV channels, and newspapers.

6.15 Curry Industry:

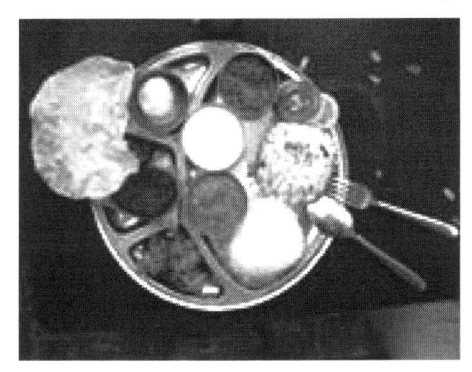

Today many of the Bangladeshi community are now part of the Curry Industry in Britain, more than 8 out of 10 Indian restaurants in the UK are owned by Bangladeshis. The number of restaurants owned by Bangladeshis increased rapidly years after years. In 1946, there were 20 restaurants or small cafes which were owned by Bengalis;

then in 1960 there were 300 owned; and by 1980, more than 3,000 have been created by them.

Now, as of today, there are 8,500 Indian restaurants, of which around 7,200 are Bangladeshi. One of the main dishes in those restaurants, the chicken tikka masala, is now regarded as Britain's national food dish. The curry industry is seen as a great success for Bangladeshis living in Britain, the industry which changed the culture of food in British cuisine.

The Chicken tikka masala is now served in restaurants around the globe, and a UK survey claimed it is the country's most popular restaurant dish. One in seven curries sold in the UK is a chicken tikka. The popularity of the dish leads the UK Foreign Minister to proclaim it as Britain's true national dish, the former prime minister, Tony Blair also recognised it as the favourite dish, by eating at a Bangladeshi curry restaurant for his daughter's birthday.

The curry industry turns over up to £4 billion a year and is viewed as recognition of Bangladeshi success, through awards such as 'The British Curry Awards. Brick Lane, known as Bangla Town, is home to many of these restaurants and is now regarded as London's 'curry capital', with thousands of visitors every day. The restaurants serve different types of curry dishes, including fish, chutneys, and other halal dishes.

Although the curry industry has been the primary business of Bangladeshis, many other Bangladeshis own grocery stores. Whitechapel is a thriving local street market, offering many low-priced goods for the local Bengali community. In Brick Lane, there are many Bengali staples available, such as frozen fish and jack fruits. There are also many travel agents offering flights to Sylhet.

Many Bangladeshi businesses located in the East End wish to maintain a link with Sylhet, for example, the weekly Sylheti Dak or the Sylhet Stores. There are also many money transfer companies;in 2007 a firm called, First Solution Money Transfer went into liquidation. Company chairman, Dr. Fazal Mahmood, admitted the business owed hundreds of thousands of pounds to the public and claimed that the firm had lost control of the money it handled due to a lack of regulation. Other large companies include Seamark and Ibco, owned by millionaire Iqbal Ahmed, Taj Stores, and many others.

In April 2008 restaurants owned by Bangladeshis came under threat. Many of those who work in these businesses are recent immigrants legally brought in from outside the UK. The British government announced it would change immigration laws for these workers, blocking access for high skilled chefs from Bangladesh. The law demanded these workers speak fluent English and have good formal qualifications to meet the requirements of society and work in Britain.

These laws have not only affected Bangladeshis but have hit other migrant workers from China and India. However, the legislation may have a particularly dramatic effect on Bangladeshis because so many of them rely heavily on the curry business. It has been estimated that 30% of their restaurant businesses are seriously threatened by these new laws.

On 20 April 2008, 44,000 people gathered and protested in London, including Bangladeshis, Chinese and Indians, and other groups who were unhappy with the changes to the law. They argued their contribution to the economy of the United Kingdom meant they deserved better treatment.

6.16 Bangladeshi Cuisine:

Bangladesh was the eastern part of Bengal before the Partition of India. The Bangladeshi cuisine incorporates many Persian-Arabic elements and the usage of beef greatly sets it apart from the cuisine in West Bengal in India. It also has considerable regional variations.

A staple across the country however is rice, various kinds of lentil, which is locally known as dal (sometimes written as daal) & fish. As a large percentage of the land (over 80% on some occasions) can be underwater, either intentionally because of farming practices or due to severe climatologically, topographical or geographical conditions, not surprisingly fish features as a major source of protein in the Bangladeshi diet. There is also a saying which goes, "Machh-e-Bhat-e-Bangali" (Fish and rice make a Bengali).

An integral part of Bangladeshi cuisine is mutton, the presence of which is a must, especially in feasts and banquets. Kabab from mutton is immensely popular throughout the country. Mutton is used in the preparation of a wide range of dishes including biryani, tehari, haleem, and many others. Regional feasts such as the Mezbaan and Ziafat of Chittagong, Sylhet, and Comilla or the Dawat of Dhaka will remain incomplete without serving spicy Mutton.

Meat curry with rice
British Bangladeshis consume traditional Bangladeshi food, in particular rice with curry.Many traditional Bengali dishes are served with rice, including chicken, lentils (Dahl), and fish. Another popular food is shatkora, which is a citrus and tangy fruit from Sylhet, mainly used for flavourings in curries.Bangladeshi cooking has become popular in Britain because of the number of Bangladeshi-owned restaurants, which has increased significantly.

In 1946 there were 20 restaurants, whilst today there are 7,200 owned by Bangladeshis, out of a total of 8,500 Indian restaurants in the UK.Surveys show that Bangladeshi curries are amongst the most popular of dishes;the chicken tikka masala is now regarded as one of Britain's favourite national food dishes.

6.17 Regional Cuisines:

Bangladeshi Cuisine is a generic terminology to refer to the cooking style and trend now prevalent in Bangladesh. However, there are several regional variations, in terms of dishes, cooking style, serving style, and nomenclature. In general, for cooking purposes, the administrative divisions more or less correspond to regional divides as well.

Beef curry served with roasted onion in Dhaka, Bangladesh

The main differences are as follows:

South - Barisal Division, Chittagong Division, and Khulna Division, being close to the sea, tend to have larger use of sea fishes in their cuisines in addition to coconut. Shutki, which is an especially treated dry fish, is extremely popular in these areas. Shutki is also exported from these regions. Dishes especially involving beef and lentils are characteristic of Mezbaan feasts in Chittagong Division. Beef is rarely seen in Barisal or Khulna.

Dhaka/Central - Dishes involving spiced rice and a lot of meat are usually legacies of Dhaka's past as the capital of the Bengali empires. Much of this is still visible in the old city, where dishes like Biryani, different types of Kabab,

Mughlai Parata, and Bakar Khani are made by specialty stores, many of which have existed for over a century.

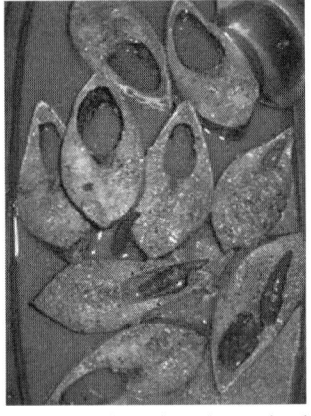

Shorshe Elish, a dish of smoked Elish with mustard seeds, has been an important part of both Bangladeshi and Bengali cuisine.

West and North-west - Vegetable curries heavily occupy the main eating in these areas. Also, spices are more common, and more heavily, used. River fishes (sweet water fishes) are common in the dishes. North-east - A large number of lakes around the Sylhet Division encourages greater use of lake fishes in the cuisine. Because of proximity to the hills in Assam, several fruits and pickles that are otherwise absent in the rest of the country, such as shatkora are used in cooking and serving, producing a distinct nature to the dining menu here.

Phuchka - an enormously popular spicy snack

Alu Bhaji occurs across the region. Lucchi, a flatbread.

Shujir Halua semolina-based halua from across the region.

Fuchka a variant of a popular spicy snack.

6.18 Staple Ingredients and Spices:

The staples of Bangladeshi cuisine are rice, atta (a special type of whole wheat flour), and at least five dozen varieties of pulses, the most important of which are chana (Bengal gram), tur (pigeon pea or red gram), urod (black gram), and mung (green gram). Pulses are used almost exclusively in the form of dal, except chana, which is often cooked whole for breakfast and is processed into flour (beshon).

However, unlike neighbouring Indian food that includes types of rice and bread, the main source of carbohydrates in a "regular" Bangladeshi meal is plain white rice. Different kinds of fried rice, in the form of pulao and biriyani, are eaten mainly on special occasions and at parties.

Bangladeshi food varies between very 'sweet' and mild-to extremely spicy; many tourists even from other Southeast Asian and Subcontinental countries find the food spicy. It resembles North-East Indian and Southeast Asian food more closely than that of any other part of the Subcontinent, most likely due to geographic and cultural proximity. The most important flavours in Bangladeshi cuisine are garlic, ginger, lime, coriander, cumin, turmeric, andchili. In sweet dishes, cardamom and cinnamon are amongst the natural flavors.

6.19   Other famous Bangladeshi dishes

Torkari
Biryani Kachchi (mutton) Biriyani, Chicken Biriyani & Tehari (beef).
Khichuri (rice cooked with lentils)

There are several styles of Bangladeshi bread, including Luchi, Nan, Tandoori roti, chapati, and paratha.

6.20   Sweets and desserts:

Varieties of pithas (Pakan, Pati Shapta, etc.)
Bangladeshi cuisine has a rich tradition of sweets. The most common sweets and desserts include –

- Chômchôm Tangail's Porabarir chomchom is famous
- Kalo jam - Flour, Sugar, Milk mixed with special spice.
- Golap Jam - Flour, Sugar, and Milk mixed with special spice.
- Rosho-Golla - Flour, Sugar, and Milk mixed with special spice.
- A wide variety of Pitha - steamed rice cakes or Vape Pitha, Chitoi Pitha, Pan Pitha.
- Firni also known as Payesh
- Khir – Sweet Rice Putin
- Halua- there are different types of halua (semolina - Shuji, carrot - gajor, almond - badam, boot, etc)
- Jilapi – Flour, Sugar, fried in Oil.
- Doi - Sweetened Creamy Yoghurt
- Shemai - sweet vermicelli in cinnamon, cardamom, and star anise infused milk.

- Sandesh - in Bangladesh, this is a palm sugar and rice flour fritter unlike the Sandesh of West Bengal
- Chhana - also known as Kacha Shondesh, is an unrefined form of Sandesh
- Jorda - sweetened rice or vermicelli, fried in ghee (clarified butter)
- Shon-papri- Sweet Gram Flour Noodles, very fine delicate with a melt-in-the-mouth texture.
- Rosh-malai - small roshogollas in a sweetened milk base; Comilla is famous for its Roshmalai.
- Khaja & Goja - fried sweets
- Barfi - there are different kinds of them
- Murob-ba - traditionally made Bengali succade with various fruits such as Lime, Citron, Papaya, Mango, Pineapple, Soursop, Watermelon and also Ginger

6.21 Beverages

Borhani (a spiced Mughal drink made from yogurt with various eastern spice), it is generally drunk with biryani or another rich meal.
Tea

6.22 Local businesses:

Many other Bangladeshis own grocery stores are situated in many towns and cities. The store offers many products and foods including fish, meat, and exotic vegetable. There are many Bengali staples available such as jack fruit, betel nut, and paan leaves, and frozen fish.

Various travel agents offer many flights to Sylhet with the national airline, Biman Bangladesh Airlines, for around £550.

Every Bangladeshi business located in the Greater Manchester area seems to hark back to the city of Sylhet, Surma Housing Association, Shahjalal Housing Association, Shahjalal Mosque, Jalalabad Jameh Mosque, and Sylhet Welfare Association.

One of the most well-known stores and brands of Bangladeshi products is Seamark and Ibco, owned by millionaire Iqbal Ahmed and it has food delivered from all over the world with many products. Founded in 1984, Iqbal Brothers is one of the oldest international grocers in the UK and situated in Manchester. Seamark and Ibco have a long tradition in serving the business as well as the local community in England and Europe with only the finest quality seasonal produce, flown daily from Bangladesh. There are also hundreds of fast-food stores scattered across Greater Manchester, owned by Bangladeshis.

They are also the suppliers of quality goods, fresh food produce, and spices to retailers, wholesalers, shipping agents, caterers, and the general public, throughout Manchester. It offers people huge selections of freshly prepared food products from the world palate, for example, items such as Naan, prawn crackers, pitta-breads, samosa to delicious exotic sweets, beverages, halal meat, fresh fish, and many more Bangladesh products.

6.23   Media:

People have gone beyond by working in media, where the first Bangladeshi channel abroad was created called Bangla TV in 1999, and later other channels emerged, these are called Channel S in 2004, ATN Bangla UK in 2005, Channel I Europe in October 2007, NTV in 2008, Desh TV in 2011 and Channel Nine UK in April 2012. These channels broadcast programmes, with many talk shows offering advice from lawyers and barristers such as 'Legal Advice', talk shows, Bengali film and entertainment, an Islamic voice for the community.

Also, Bangla news published from London is Weekly Surma, Notun Din, Jonomot, Euro Bangla, Potrika, London Bangla, Bangla Post, Bangladesh, Jumabar, daily Amader Protidin, Probashe Protidin, etc.

6.24   Remittance:

Many other Bangladeshis are sending money to Bangladesh to build luxury types of houses, whereas in the United Kingdom many are living in poverty, facing deprivation, and spending less. In many villages in Sylhet, there are large numbers of luxury homes built in some suburbs or communities, the financial support mainly sent from the UK. So many are returning to build homes in Bangladesh that they are fuelling a building boom in Sylhet.

Businesses have also been established by the British expatriates in the city of Sylhet, such as hotels, restaurants, often themed on those found in London, have also been established to cater to the visiting Sylheti expatriate population and the growing Sylheti middle classes (i.e. London Fried Chicken or Tessco).

The financial relationship between British Bengalis and relatives in Bangladesh has changed, only 20% of Bangladeshi families in east London were sending money to Bangladesh as of 1995, this figure was approximately 85% during the 1960-70s. For a large number of families in Britain the cost of living, housing, or education for the children severely constrains any regular financial commitment towards Bangladesh.

Moreover, the family reunion process has resulted in the social and economic reproduction of the household in Britain; conflicts over land or money can arise involving the mutual or reciprocal relationship between members of a joint household divided by migration. This, in turn, can reduce even more the level of investment in Sylhet.

The emergence of a second and the third generation of British Bangladeshis is another factor explaining the declining proportion of people's income being sent as remittances to Bangladesh. About 30% of all remittances sent to Bangladesh are from Britain as of 1987.

6.25 Conclusion:

Rather than studying a particular place, we decided to look at people from all sectors. This allowed us to explore some of the smaller communities of Bangladeshis living in the Greater Manchester area and also to get a sense of how the Bangladeshi community in Britain is changing and becoming more scattered. For this part of our research, we interviewed people in Hyde, Aston-under-Lyne, Oldham, Rochdale, Manchester, and Chester. Please see chapter 8 for details.

Chapter 7 - Greater Manchester Communities

Northwest England, informally known as The Northwest, is one of the nine official regions of England.

Northwest England had a 2006 estimated population of 6,853,201 the third most populated region after London and the Southeast. According to the 2011 census the total population is 7,052,177.The Northwest comprises five ceremonial counties of England – Cumbria, Lancashire, Greater Manchester, Merseyside, and Cheshire.

Northwest England is bounded to the east by the Peak District and the Pennines and the west by the Irish Sea. The region extends from the Scottish Borders in the north to the northern margins of the English Midlands in the south. To its southwest is North Wales. Amongst the better known of the North West's physiographical features in the Lake District and the Cheshire Plain. The highest point in Northwest England (and the highest peak in England) is Scafell Pike, Cumbria, at a height of 3,209 feet (978 m).

A mix of a rural and urban landscape, two large conurbations, centered on Liverpool and Manchester, occupy much of the south of the region. The north of the region, comprising Cumbria and northern Lancashire, is largely rural, as is the far south which encompasses parts of the Cheshire Plain and Peak District.

These Bar Charts show the recent percentage of people living within Greater Manchester and Bangladeshis living within Greater Manchester.

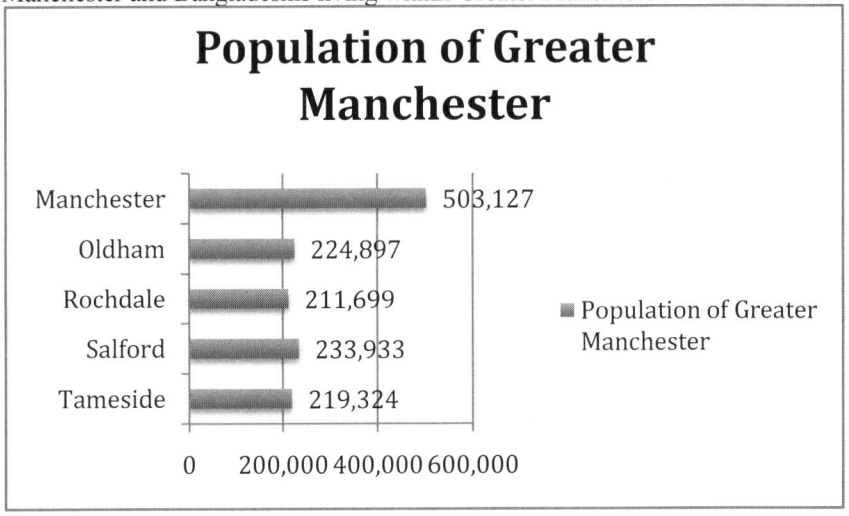

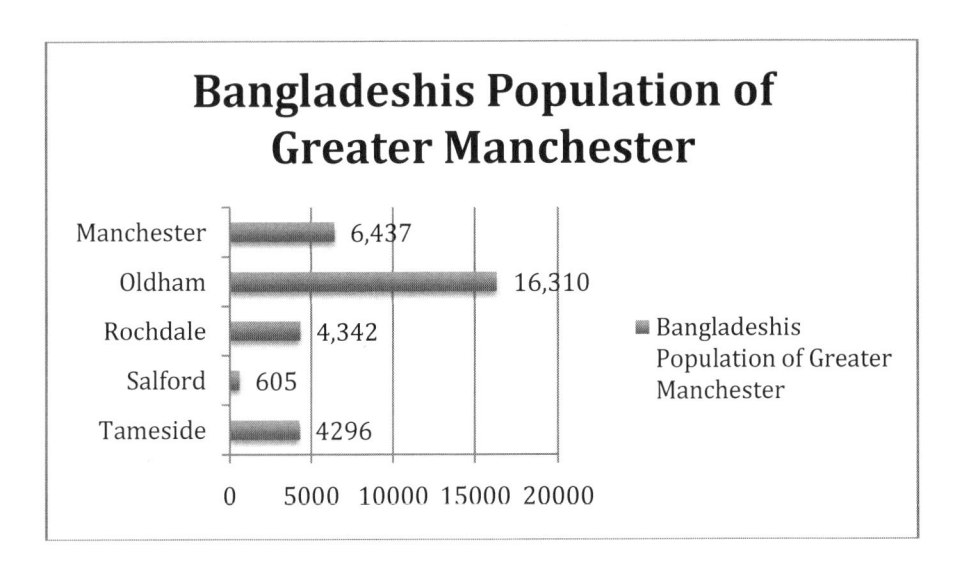

Population of Greater Manchester

District	Population
Manchester	503,127
Oldham	224,897
Rochdale	211,699
Salford	233,933
Tameside	219,324

Bangladeshis Population of Greater Manchester

District	Population
Manchester	6,437
Oldham	16,310
Rochdale	4,342
Salford	605
Tameside	4296

7.1- Greater Manchester:

Greater Manchester is a metropolitan county in North West England, with a population of 2.6 million. It encompasses one of the largest metropolitan areas in the United Kingdom and comprises ten metropolitan boroughs: Bolton, Bury, Oldham, Rochdale, Stockport, Tameside, Trafford, Wigan, and the cities of Manchester and Salford. Greater Manchester was created on 1 April 1974 as a result of the Local Government Act 1972.

Greater Manchester spans 493 square miles (1,277 km2). It is landlocked and borders Cheshire (to the south-west and south), Derbyshire (to the south-east), West Yorkshire (to the north-east), Lancashire (to the north), and Merseyside (to the west). There is a mix of high-density urban areas, suburbs, semi-rural and rural locations in Greater Manchester, but overwhelmingly the land use is urban. It has a focused central business district, formed by Manchester city centre and the adjoining parts of Salford and Trafford, but Greater Manchester is also a polycentric county with ten metropolitan districts, each of which has at least one major town centre and outlying suburbs. The Greater Manchester Urban Area is the third most populous conurbation in the UK and spans most of the county's territory.

For the 12 years following 1974, the county had a two-tier system of local government; district councils shared power with the Greater Manchester County Council. The county council was abolished in 1986, and so its districts (the metropolitan boroughs) effectively became unitary authority areas. However, the metropolitan county has continued to exist in law and as a geographic frame of reference, and as a ceremonial county, has a Lord Lieutenant and a High Sheriff. Several county-wide services were coordinated through the Association of Greater Manchester Authorities up until April 2011, when the Greater Manchester Combined Authority was established as the strategic county-wide authority for Greater Manchester, taking on functions and responsibilities for economic development, regeneration, and transport.

Before the creation of the metropolitan county, the name SELNEC was used for the area, taken from the initials of "Southeast Lancashire Northeast Cheshire". Greater Manchester is an amalgamation of 70 former local government districts from the former administrative counties of Lancashire, Cheshire, the West Riding of Yorkshire, and eight independent county boroughs.

7.1.1 - History

The history of Manchester encompasses its change from a minor Lancastrian township into the pre-eminent industrial metropolis of the United Kingdom and the world. Manchester began expanding "at an astonishing rate" around the turn of the 19th century as part of a process of unplanned urbanization brought on by a boom in textile manufacture during the Industrial Revolution. The transformation took little more than a century.

Evolving from a Roman Cestrum in Celtic Britain, Manchester was the site of the world's first passenger railway station and many scientific achievements of great importance. Manchester also led the political and economic reform of 19th-century Britain as the vanguard of free trade. The mid-20th century saw a decline in Manchester's industrial importance, prompting a depression in social and economic conditions. Subsequent investment, gentrification, and rebranding from the 1990s onwards changed its fortunes and reinvigorated Manchester as a post-industrial city with multiple sporting, broadcasting, and educational institutions.

During the late 19th century Manchester began to suffer an economic decline, partly exacerbated by its reliance on the Port of Liverpool, which was charging excessive dock usage fees. Championed by local industrialist Daniel Adamson, the Manchester Ship Canal was built as a way to reverse this. It gave the city direct access to the sea allowing it to export its manufactured goods directly. This meant that it no longer had to rely on the railways and Liverpool's ports. When completed in 1894 it allowed Manchester to become Britain's third busiest port, despite being 40 miles (64 km) inland. The Manchester Ship Canal was created by canalising the Rivers Irwell and Mersey for 36 miles (58 km) from Salford to the Mersey estuary at the port of Liverpool. This enabled ocean-going ships to sail right into the Port of Manchester Docks (technically in Salford). The docks functioned until the 1970s, when their closure led to a large increase in unemployment in the area.

Trafford Park in Stretford (outside the city boundaries) was the world's first industrial estate and still exists today, though with a significant tourist and recreational presence. Manchester suffered greatly from the inter-war depression and the underlying structural changes that began to supplant the old industries, including textile manufacture.

World War II
In the Second World War Manchester played a key role as an industrial manufacturing city, including the Avro aircraft factory (now BAE Systems) which built countless aircraft for the RAF, the most famous being the Avro Lancaster bomber. As a consequence of its war efforts, the city suffered heavily from bombing during The Blitz from 1940 to 1941. It was attacked several times by the Luftwaffe, particularly in the "Christmas Blitz" of 1940, which destroyed a large part of the historic city centre and seriously damaged the Cathedral.

Post-war
The Royal Exchange ceased trading in 1968. The 1950s saw the start of Manchester's rise as a football superpower. Despite the Munich air disaster, Manchester United F.C. went on to become one of the world's most famous clubs, rising to a dominance of the English game in the 1990s.

Mancunian Films had been established by John E. Blakeley in the 1930s as a vehicle for northern comedians such as George Formby and Frank. The company opened its studios in Manchester in 1947 and produced a successful sequence of films until Blakeley's retirement six years later. The studio was sold to the BBC in 1954 which was the same year that saw the advent of commercial television in the UK. The establishment of Granada Television based in the city attracted much of the production talent from the studios and continued Manchester's tradition of cultural innovation, often with its trademark social radicalism in its programming.

The same period saw the rise of national celebrity of local stars from the Granada TV soap opera Coronation Street and footballers such as George.

As with many British cities during the period, the 1950s and 1960s saw extensive re-development of the city, with old and overcrowded housing cleared to make way for high-rise blocks of flats. This changed the appearance of Manchester considerably, although the high-rise experiment later proved unpopular and unsuccessful. The city centre also saw major re-development, with developments such as the Manchester Arndale.

Manchester's key role in the industrial revolution was repeated and the city became a centre of research and development. Manchester made important contributions to the computer revolution. The father of modern computing Alan Turing was based at Manchester University and it was his idea of the stored program concept that lead in 1948 to The Manchester Small-Scale Experimental Machine, nicknamed Baby, which was the first stored-program computer to run a program. This was developed by Frederic C. Williams and Tom Kilburn at the University of Manchester. This was followed by The Manchester Mark 1, in 1949. These inventions were commercialised in the Ferranti Mark 1, one of the first commercially available computers.

In 1974, Manchester was split from the county of Lancashire, and the Metropolitan Borough of Manchester was created.
The diversification of the city's economy helped to cushion the blow of this decline. However, as with many inner-city areas, the growth of car ownership and commuting meant that many people moved from the inner-city and into surrounding suburbs. By 1971 the population of Manchester had declined to 543,868, and by 2001 422,302.

In 2002, the city hosted the XVII Commonwealth Games very successfully, earning praise from many previously sceptical sources. Manchester has twice failed in its bid to host the Olympic Games, losing to Atlanta in 1996 and Sydney in 2000.

In the 1990s, Manchester earned a reputation for gang-related crime, particularly after a spate of shootings involving young men, and reports of teenagers carrying handguns as "fashion accessories". Gun crime is still a problem in Manchester and several initiatives are in place by the Greater Manchester Police in an attempt to reduce the number of youths getting involved with gangs and their associated crimes. However, the success of this is questionable as gun crime in the area is still increasing and is at a level significantly above comparable areas of the UK. The district of Moss Side gained a particular reputation for gang violence and has seen the substantial community and police initiatives attempting to rejuvenate the area. In 2004 anti-social behaviour orders were widely used to combat minor crimes.

The Canal Street area of the city is well known as the "Gay Village". Manchester's claim to the status of the "gay capital of the UK" was strengthened in 2003 when it played host city to the annual Euro pride festival.

During the 1980s, the Victoria University of Manchester had somewhat complacently exploited its reputation as one of the leading red brick universities. During the same period, many of those universities established post-war vigorously pursued policies of growth and innovation. The university consequently saw its standing decline and only in the 1990s did it embark on a catch-up programme. In October 2004 the Victoria University of Manchester and UMIST merged to form the University of Manchester, the largest University in the UK with ambitious plans to be one of the world's leading research-intensive universities.

Since the regeneration after the 1996 IRA bomb, and aided by the XVII Commonwealth Games, Manchester's city centre has changed significantly. Large sections of the city dating from the 1960s have been either demolished and re-developed or modernised with the use of glass and steel; a good example of this transformation is the Manchester Arndale.
Many old mills and textile warehouses have been converted into apartments, helping to give the city a much more modern, upmarket look and feel. Some areas, like Hulme, have undergone extensive regeneration programmes and many million-pound Lofthouse apartments have since been developed to cater to its growing business community. The 168 meters tall, 47-story Beetham Tower, completed in 2006, provides the highest residential accommodation in the United Kingdom - the lower 23 floors form the Hilton Hotel, while the upper 24 floors are apartments. The Beetham Tower was originally planned to stand 171 meters in height, but this had to be changed due to local wind conditions.

Parts of the city centre were affected by rioting by Rangers fans during the 2008 UEFA Cup Final riots.

As of 2011, Manchester and Salford are on a tentative list for UNESCO World Heritage Site status. The proposal centres on the Bridgewater Canal, regarded as the first true canal which helped create the industrial revolution.

On Tuesday 9 August 2011 the centres of Manchester and Salford were affected by the 2011 England riots: see Timeline of 2011 England riots. Tuesday, 9th August.

City of Manchester

In 1853 the Borough was elevated to City status. In 1885 further areas were added to the City of Manchester with Bradford, Harpurhey, Rusholme, and parts of Moss Side and Withington townships.

By the Local Government Act 1888, the City of Manchester became in 1889 a County Borough, although it still kept the city title.

Other areas, which had been under the control of Lancashire County Council, were added to the City between 1890 and 1933:

1890: Blackley, Crumpsall, Moston, Openshaw, and Newton (incl. Kirkmanshulme) townships, Clayton area (part of Droylsden township), and part of Gorton township.

1901: A very small part of Gorton Urban District.
1903: Part (Heaton Park area) of Prestwich Urban District.
1904: Burnage, Didsbury, and Chorlton-cum-Hardy civil parishes and Moss Side and Withington Urban Districts.
1909: Levenshulme Urban District and the remaining area of Gorton Urban District.
1913: Part of Heaton Norris Urban District.
1933: Part of Denton Urban District.

In addition to these areas, in 1931 the Cheshire civil parishes of Baguley, Northenden, and Northen Etchells were also added to the City of Manchester.

Under the Local Government Act 1972, the City of Manchester, with the addition of the civil parish of Ringway, became on 1 April 1974 one of the ten Metropolitan Boroughs of the newly created Metropolitan County of Greater Manchester.

In 1986 Greater Manchester County Council was abolished by the Local Government Act 1985 and most of its functions were devolved to the ten boroughs, making them effectively unitary authorities. Some of the County Council's functions were taken over by joint bodies such as a passenger transport authority, and joint fire, police, and waste disposal authorities.

In one of its most noted acts, Manchester City Council carried a resolution in 1980 to create the UK's first Nuclear Free Zone. The Peace Gardens were later constructed on a small piece of land in St. Peters Square.

Before 1974 the area of Greater Manchester was split between Cheshire and Lancashire with numerous parts being independent county boroughs. The area was informally known as "SELNEC", for "South East Lancashire North East Cheshire". Also, small parts of the West Riding of Yorkshire (around Saddle worth) and Derbyshire were covered.

SELNEC had been proposed by the Redcliffe-Maud Report of 1969 as a "metropolitan area". This had roughly the same northern boundary as today's Greater Manchester but covered much more territory in northeast Cheshire – including Macclesfield and Warrington. It also covered Glossop in Derbyshire.

In 1969 a SELNEC Passenger Transport Authority was set up, which covered an area smaller than the proposed SELNEC, but different from the eventual Greater Manchester.

Although the Redcliffe-Maud report was rejected by the Conservative Party government after it won the 1970 general election, it was committed to local government reform and accepted the need for a county-based in Manchester. Its original proposal was much smaller than the Redcliffe-Maud Report's SELNEC, but further fringe areas such as Wilmslow, Warrington, and Glossop were trimmed from the edges and included instead in the shire counties. The metropolitan county of Greater Manchester was eventually established in 1974.

Greater Manchester's representative county council was abolished in 1986, following the Local Government Act 1985. However, Greater Manchester is still a metropolitan county and ceremonial county.

7.1.2 - Industrial Revolution

Manchester remained a small market town until the late 18th century and the beginning of the Industrial. Some sources define the start of the industrial revolution as July 1761, when the Duke reached Castle field. The myriad small valleys in the Pennine Hills to the north and east of the town, combined with the damp climate, proved ideal for the construction of water-powered Cotton mills such as Quarry Bank Mill, which industrialised the spinning and weaving of cloth.

Indeed, it was the importation of cotton, which began towards the end of the eighteenth century that revolutionised the textile industry in the area. This new commodity was imported through the port of Liverpool, which was connected with Manchester by the Mersey and Irwell Navigation - the two rivers had been made navigable from the 1720s onwards.

Manchester is now developed as the natural distribution centre for raw cotton and spun yarn and a marketplace and distribution centre for the products of this growing textile industry. Arkwright is credited as the first to erect a cotton mill in the city. His first experiment, installing a Newcomen steam engine to pump water for a waterwheel failed, but he next adapted a Watt steam engine to directly operate the machinery. The result was the rapid spread of cotton mills throughout Manchester itself and in the surrounding towns. To these must be added bleach works, textile print works, and the engineering workshops and foundries, all serving the cotton industry. During the mid 19th century Manchester grew to become the centre of Lancashire's cotton industry and was dubbed "Cotton polis", and a branch of the Bank of England was established in 1826. The prosperity of the textile industry leads to an expansion of Manchester and the surrounding conurbation. Many institutions were established including Belle Vue leisure gardens and zoo (founded by John Jennison in 1836), the Manchester Athenaeum (1836–1837), the Corn Exchange(1837), and the Royal Victoria Gallery of Practical Science (1840–42).
This wealth fuelled the development of science and education in Manchester. The Manchester Academy had relocated to York in 1803 and, though it returned in 1840, in 1853 it moved again to London, eventually becoming Harris Manchester College, Oxford. However, a Mechanics' Institute, later to become UMIST, was founded in 1824 by among others, John Dalton the "father of atomic theory". In 1851 Owens College was founded by the trustees of John Owens, a textile merchant who had left a bequest for that purpose. Owens College was to become the first constituent college of the Victoria University (UK) which was granted its Royal Charter in 1880.

The growth of the city government continued with Manchester finally being incorporated as a borough in 1838, covering what is now the city centre, along with Cheetham, Beswick, Ardwick, Chorlton upon Medlock, and Hulme.

In 1841, Robert Angus Smith took up work as an analytical chemist at the Royal Manchester Institution and started to research unprecedented environmental problems. Smith went on to become the first director of the Alkali Inspectorate and to characterise, and coin the term, acid rain.

Manchester continued to be a nexus of political radicalism. From 1842 to 1844, the German social philosopher Friedrich Engels lived there and wrote his influential book Condition of the Working Class in England (1845). He habitually met Karl Marx in an alcove at Chetham's Library.

In 1846 the Borough bought the manorial rights from the Mosley family and the granting of city status followed in 1853. In 1847 the Manchester diocese of the Church of England was established. In 1851, the Borough became the first local authority to seek water supplies beyond its boundaries. By 1853, the number of cotton mills in Manchester had reached its peak of 108.

The Cooperative Wholesale Society was formed in 1862. The outbreak of the American Civil War in 1861 saw an immediate shortage of cotton and the ensuing cotton famine brought enormous distress to the area until the war ended in 1865. The first Trades Union Congress was held in Manchester (at the Mechanics' Institute, David Street), from 2 to 6 June 1868. Manchester was the subject of Friedrich Engels' the Condition of the Working Class in England in 1844, Engels himself spending much of his life in and around Manchester. Manchester was also an important cradle of the Labour Party and the Suffragette Movement.

Manchester's golden age was perhaps the last quarter of the 19th century. Many great public buildings (including the Town Hall) date from the 19th century. The city's cosmopolitan atmosphere contributed to a vibrant culture, which included the Hallé Orchestra. In 1889, when county councils were created in England, the municipal borough became a county borough with even greater autonomy.

Cotton mills in Ancoats in 1820.

7.1.3 - Growth of the textile trade

By the sixteenth century, the wool trade had made Manchester a flourishing market town. The collegiate church, which is now the Cathedral, was finally completed in 1500–1510. The magnificently carved choir stalls date from this period, and in 1513 work began on a chapel endowed by James Stanley, Bishop of Ely, in thanksgiving for the safe return of his kinsman (sometimes said to be his son) John Stanley from the Battle of Flodden.

The English Reformation resulted in the collegiate church being rebounded as a Protestant institution. One of the more famous Wardens of this institution at the time was Dr. John Dee, known as "Queen Elizabeth's Merlin".

The town's growth was given further impetus in 1620 with the start of fustian weaving. In this period Manchester grew heavily due to an influx of Flemish settlers who founded Manchester's new weaving industry. In the 17th century, thanks to the development of the textile industry and contacts with the City of London, Manchester became a noted centre of Puritanism. Consequently, it sided with Parliament in the quarrel with Charles I. Indeed, it might be said that the War started here. In 1642, Lord Strange, the son of the Earl of Derby attempted to seize the militia magazine stored in the old College building. In the ensuing scuffle, Richard Percival, a linen weaver, was killed. He is reckoned by some to be the first casualty in the English Civil War.

Lord Strange returned and attempted to besiege the town, which had no permanent fortifications. With the help of John Rosworm, a German mercenary, the town was vigorously defended. Captain Bradshaw and his musketeers resolutely manned the bridge to Salford. Eventually, Strange realised that his force was ill-prepared, and after hearing that his father had died, withdrew to claim his title.

During the Commonwealth, Manchester was granted a seat in Parliament for the first time. Maj Gen Charles Worsley, scion of an old Lancashire family and one of Cromwell's most trusted lieutenants, had been given the Mace at the famous dissolution of Parliament in 1654. Elected Manchester's first MP, he did not sit for long before Parliament was again dissolved, leading to the Rule of the Major Generals: effectively martial law. Worsley, given responsibility for Lancashire, Cheshire, and Staffordshire, took his duties seriously, turning out ale houses, banning bear-baiting, and cracking down on the celebration of Christmas. He eventually died in 1656, at a time of the gradual ebbing away of Cromwell's authority.

On the English Restoration in 1660, as a reprisal for its defense of the Parliamentarian cause, Manchester was deprived of its recently granted Members of Parliament. No MP was to sit for Manchester until 1832. The consequences of the restoration led to a great deal of soul searching. One clergyman, Henry Newcombe, could not remain in the remodeled Anglican Church and was instrumental in the establishment of the Cross Street Chapel in 1694. This later passed into Unitarian hands, and a new chapel on the original site can be visited.

Humphrey Chetham purchased the old College buildings after the Civil War and endowed them as a bluecoat school. Chetham's Hospital, as it was known, later became Chetham's School of Music. The endowment included a collection of books, which in 1653 became Chetham's Library, the first free public library in the English-speaking world. As of 2007, it is still open and free to use.

Despite the political setbacks, the town continued to prosper. Many inhabitants supported the Glorious Revolution in 1688. They became discontented with the Tory clergy at the collegiate church, and a separate church, more to their tastes, was founded by Lady Ann Bland. St Ann's Church is a fine example of an early Georgian church and was consecrated in 1712. The surroundings, what is now St Ann's Square but was previously known as Acres field, were in imitation of a London square.

About this time, Defoe described the place as "the greatest mere village in England", by which he meant that a place the size of a populous market town had no form of local government to speak of, and was still subject to the whims of a lord of the manor.

In 1745, Charles Edward Stuart and his army entered Manchester en route to London. Despite its previous radicalism, the town offered no resistance and the Jacobites obtained enough recruits to form a 'Manchester Regiment'. It is suggested that this was because the town had no local government to speak of, and the magistrates, who could have organised resistance, were mostly conservative landowners. Moreover, these Tory landowners had taken to apprenticing their sons to Manchester merchants, so the political complexion of the town's elite had changed. The Jacobite army got no further than Derby and then retreated. On their way back through Manchester, the stragglers were pelted by the mob. The luckless 'Manchester Regiment' was left behind to garrison Carlisle, where they quickly surrendered to the pursuing British Army.

7.1.4 - Population

Manchester's population exploded as people moved from the surrounding countryside, and other parts of the British Isles, into the city seeking new opportunities. Particularly large numbers also came from Ireland, especially after the Potato Famine of the 1840s. The Irish influence continues to this day and, every March Manchester plays host to a large St Patrick's Day parade. It is estimated that about 35% of the population of Manchester and Salford has at least some Irish ancestry.

Large numbers of (mostly Jewish) immigrants later came to Manchester from central and Eastern Europe. The area, including Salford and Prestwich, today has a Jewish population of about 40,000. This is the largest Jewish community outside London in quite some way. To these groups may be added (in later years) Levantines (involved in the Egyptian cotton trade), Germans, and Italians. By the end of the nineteenth century, Manchester was a very cosmopolitan place. The most recent census which is 2009 has stated that there are 483,800 living in Britain and that there are 6,700 Bangladeshis within Britain.

7.1.5 - Demography

The United Kingdom Census 2001 showed a total resident population for Manchester of 392,819, a 9.2% decline from the 1991 census. Approximately 83,000 were aged under 16, 285,000 were aged 16–74, and 25,000 aged 75 and over. According to the 2001 census, 85.2% of Manchester's population claim they have been born in the UK. Inhabitants of Manchester are known as Mancunians or Mancs for short. The census also revealed that Manchester had the second-lowest proportion of the population in the employment of any local authority in the UK. In part, this was due to the high proportion of students as Manchester had the highest proportion of students amongst local authorities. A 2007 report noted, "60 percent of Manchester people are living in some of the UK's most deprived areas".

Historically the population of Manchester began to increase rapidly during the Victorian era, peaking at 766,311 in 1931. From then the population began to decrease rapidly, due to slum clearance and the increased building of social housing overspill estates by Manchester City Council after the Second World War such as Hattersley and Langley.

The inhabitants of Manchester, as of many other large cities, are religiously diverse. At the time of the 2001 census, 62.4% of the city's population were Christian, and 9.1% Muslim. Other religions represented less than 1% each. The proportion of people without a religion (16%) was above the national average (14.8%), with 9.7% not stating their religion. The Jewish population is second only to London, and Greater Manchester also has one of the largest Muslim populations.

The percentage of the population in Manchester who reported themselves as living in the same household in a same-sex relationship was 0.4%, compared to the English national average of 0.2%.

In terms of districts by ethnic diversity, the City of Manchester is ranked highest in Greater Manchester and 34th in England. Estimates from 2005 state 77.6% of people as 'White' (71.0% of residents as White British, 3.0% White Irish, 3.6% as Other White – although those of mixed European and British ancestry is unknown, there are over 25,000 Mancunians of Italian descent alone which represents 5.5% of the city's population). 3.2% as Mixed race (1.3% Mixed White and Black Caribbean, 0.6% Mixed White and Black African, 0.7% Mixed White and Asian, 0.7% Other Mixed). 10.3% of the city's population are South Asian (2.3% Indian, 5.8% Pakistani, 1.0% Bangladeshi, 1.2% Other South Asian).

5.2% are Black (2.0% Black Caribbean, 2.7% Black African, and 0.5% Other Black). 2.3% of the city's population is Chinese, and 1.4% is another ethnic group. Kidd identifies Moss Side, Longsight, Cheetham Hill, Rusholme, as centres of population for ethnic minorities. Manchester's Irish Festival, including a St Patrick's Day parade, is one of Europe's largest. There is also a well-established Chinatown in the city with a substantial number of oriental restaurants and Chinese supermarkets. The area also attracts large numbers of Chinese students to the city, attending the local universities.

Based on population estimates for 2005, crime levels in the city were considerably higher than the national average. Some parts of Manchester were adversely affected by its rapid urbanisation, resulting in high levels of crime in areas such as Moss Side and Wythenshawe. The number of thefts from a vehicle offense and theft of a vehicle per 1,000 of the population was 25.5 and 8.9 compared to the English national average of 7.6 and 2.9 respectively. The number of sexual offenses was 1.9 compared to the average of 0.9. The national average of violence against another person was 16.7 compared to the Manchester average of 32.7. The figures for crime statistics were all recorded during the 2006/7 financial year.

The Manchester Larger Urban Zone, a Eurostat measure of the functional city-region approximated to local government districts, has a population of 2,539,100 in 2004. In addition to Manchester itself, the LUZ includes the remainder of the county of Greater Manchester. The Manchester LUZ is the second largest within the United Kingdom, behind that of London.

7.1.6 - Culture

Bands that have emerged from the Manchester music scene include The Smiths, the Buzzcocks, The Fall, Joy Division, and its successor group New Order, Oasis, Doves, and Ten. Manchester was credited as the main regional driving force behind indie bands of the 1980s including Happy Mondays, Inspiral Carpets, James, and The Stone Roses. These groups came from what became known as the "Madchester" scene that also centred on The Haçienda nightclub developed by the founder of Factory Records Tony Wilson. Although from southern England, The Chemical Brothers subsequently formed in Manchester. Ex-Stone Roses' front man Ian Brown and ex-Smiths Morrissey continue successful solo careers. Notable Manchester acts of the 1960s include The Hollies, Herman's Hermits, and the Bee Gees, who grew up in Chorlton.

Its main pop music venue is the Manchester Arena with over 21,000 seats, the largest arena of its type in Europe which has been voted International Venue of the Year. In terms of concert goers, it is the busiest indoor arena in the world ahead of Madison Square Garden in New York and the O2 Arena in London, the second and third busiest respectively. Other major venues include the Manchester Apollo and the Manchester Academy. Smaller venues are the Band on the Wall, the Roadhouse, the Night and Day Café, the Ruby Lounge, and The Deaf Institute.

Manchester has two symphony orchestras, the Hallé and the BBC Philharmonic. There is also a chamber orchestra, the Manchester Camerata. In the 1950s, the city was home to the so-called 'Manchester School' of classical composers, which comprised Harrison Birtwistle, Peter Maxwell Davies, David Ellis, and Alexander Goehr. Manchester is a centre for musical education, with the Royal Northern College of Music and Chetham's School of Music. Forerunners of the RNCM were the Northern School of Music (founded 1920) and the Royal Manchester College of Music (founded 1893). The main classical venue was the Free Trade Hall on Peter Street, until the opening in 1996 of the 2,500 seat Bridgewater Hall.

Brass band music, a tradition in the north of England, is an important part of Manchester's musical heritage; some of the UK's leading bands, such as the CWS Manchester Band and the Fairey Band, are from Manchester and surrounding areas, and the Whit Friday brass band contest takes place annually in the neighbouring areas of Saddleworth and Tameside.

7.1.7 - Economy

Manchester was at the forefront of the Industrial Revolution in the 19th-century and was a leading centre for manufacturing. The city's economy is now largely service-based and, as of 2007, is the fastest growing in the UK, with inward investment second only to the capital. Manchester's State of the City Report identifies financial and professional services, life science industries, creative, cultural and media, manufacturing, and communications as major activities. The city was ranked in 2010 as the second-best place to do business in the UK and the twelfth best in Europe.

Manchester has the largest UK office market outside London. Greater Manchester represents over £42 billion of the UK GVA, the third-largest of any English county and more than Wales or North East England.

Manchester is a focus for businesses that serve local, regional and international markets. It is the fifth-largest financial centre in the United Kingdom outside London with more than 96,300 people employed in banking, finance, and insurance. The Co-operative Group, the world's largest consumer-owned business, is based in Manchester and is one of the city's biggest employers. Legal, accounting, management consultancy, and other professional and technical services exist in Manchester.

Manchester's commercial centre is in the centre of the city, adjacent to Piccadilly, focused on Mosley Street, Deansgate, King Street and Piccadilly. Spinning fields is a £1.5 billion mixed-use development that is expanding the district west of Dean's gate. The area is designed to hold office space, retail and catering facilities, and courts. Several high-profile tenants have moved in, and a Civil Justice Centre opened in October 2007.

Manchester is the commercial, educational and cultural focus for Northwest, England, and in 2010 was ranked as the fourth biggest central retail area in the UK by sales. The city centre retail area contains shops from chain stores up to high-end boutiques such as Vivienne Westwood, Emporio Armani, DKNY, Harvey Nichols, Chanel, and Hermès.

7.1.7 - Social History

In 2002, the city hosted the XVII Commonwealth Games very successfully, earning praise from many previously skeptical sources. Manchester has twice failed in its bid to host the Olympic Games, losing to Atlanta in 1996 and Sydney in 2000.

In the 1990s, Manchester earned a reputation for gang-related crime, particularly after a spate of shootings involving young men, and reports of teenagers carrying handguns as "fashion accessories". Gun crime is still a problem in Manchester and several initiatives are in place by the Greater Manchester Police in an attempt to reduce the number of youths getting involved with gangs and their associated crimes. However, the success of this is questionable as gun crime in the area is still increasing and is at a level significantly above comparable areas of the UK. The district of Moss Side gained a particular reputation for gang violence and has seen the substantial community and police initiatives attempting to rejuvenate the area. In 2004 anti-social behaviour orders were widely used to combat minor crimes.

The Canal Street area of the city is well known as the "Gay Village". Manchester's claim to the status of the "gay capital of the UK" was strengthened in 2003 when it played host city to the annual Euro pride festival.

During the 1980s, the Victoria University of Manchester had somewhat complacently exploited its reputation as one of the leading brick universities. During the same period, many of those universities established post-war vigorously pursued policies of growth and innovation. The university consequently saw its standing decline and only in the 1990s did it embark on a catch-up programme. In October 2004 the Victoria University of Manchester and UMIST merged to form the University of Manchester, the largest University in the UK with ambitious plans to be one of the world's leading research-intensive universities.

Since the regeneration after the 1996 IRA bomb, and aided by the XVII Commonwealth Games, Manchester's city centre has changed significantly. Large sections of the city dating from the 1960s have been either demolished and re-developed or modernised with the use of glass and steel; a good example of this transformation is the Manchester Arndale. Many old mills and textile warehouses have been converted into apartments, helping to give the city a much more modern, upmarket look and feel. Some areas, like Hulme, have undergone extensive regeneration programmes and many million-pound Lofthouse apartments have since been developed to cater to its growing business community. The 168 meters tall, 47-story Beetham Tower, completed in 2006, provides the highest residential accommodation in the United Kingdom - the lower 23 floors form the Hilton Hotel, while the upper 24 floors are apartments. The Beetham Tower was originally planned to stand 171 meters in height, but this had to be changed due to local wind conditions.

Parts of the city centre were affected by rioting by Rangers fans during the 2008 UEFA Cup Final riots. As of 2011, Manchester and Salford are on a tentative list for UNESCO World Heritage Site status. The proposal centres on the Bridgewater Canal, regarded as the first true canal which helped create the industrial revolution. On Tuesday 9 August 2011 the centres of Manchester and Salford were affected by the 2011 England riots.

7.1.8 - Education

There are two universities in the City of Manchester. The University of Manchester is the largest full-time non-collegiate university in the United Kingdom and was created in 2004 by the merger of Victoria University of Manchester and UMIST. It includes the Manchester Business School, which offered the first MBA course in the UK in 1965. Manchester Metropolitan University was formed as Manchester Polytechnic on the merger of three colleges in 1970. It gained university status in 1992, and in the same year absorbed Crewe and Alsager College of Higher Education in South Cheshire.

The University of Manchester, Manchester Metropolitan University, and the Royal Northern College of Music are grouped around Oxford Road on the southern side of the city centre, which forms Europe's largest urban higher education precinct. Together they have a combined population of 73 160 students in higher education, though almost 6 000 of these were based at Manchester Metropolitan University's campuses at Crewe and Alsager in Cheshire.

One of Manchester's most notable secondary schools is the Manchester Grammar School. Established in 1515, as a free grammar school next to what is now the Cathedral, it moved in 1931 to Old Hall Lane in Fallowfield, south Manchester, to accommodate the growing student body. In the post-war period, it was a direct grant grammar school (i.e. partially state-funded), but it reverted to independent status in 1976 after the abolition of the direct-grant system. Its previous premises are now used by Chetham's School of Music. There are three schools nearby: William Hulme's Grammar School, Withington Girls' School, and Manchester High School for Girls.

In 2010, the Manchester Local Education Authority was ranked last out of Greater Manchester's ten LEAs – and 147th out of 150 in the country LEAs – based on the percentage of pupils attaining at least five A*–C grades at General Certificate of Secondary Education (GCSE) including math's and English (38.6 percent compared with the national average of 50.7 percent).

The LEA also had the highest occurrence of absences, with 11.11 percent of "half-day sessions missed by pupils", above the national average of 5.8 percent. Of the schools in the LEA with 30 or more pupils, four had

90 percent or more pupils achieving at least five A*–C grades at GCSE including math's and English (Manchester High School for Girls, St Bede's College, Manchester Islamic High School for Girls, and The King David High School) while three managed 25 percent or below (Plant Hill Arts College, North Manchester High School for Boys, Brookway High School and Sports College).

7.1.9 - Economy

Manchester was at the forefront of the Industrial Revolution in the 19th-century and was a leading centre for manufacturing. The city's economy is now largely service-based and, as of 2007, is the fastest growing in the UK, with inward investment second only to the capital. Manchester's State of the City Report identifies financial and professional services, life science industries, creative, cultural and media, manufacturing, and communications as major activities. The city was ranked in 2010 as the second-best place to do business in the UK and the twelfth best in Europe.

Manchester has the largest UK office market outside London. Greater Manchester represents over £42 billion of the UK GVA, the third-largest of any English county and more than Wales or North East England.

Manchester is a focus for businesses that serve local, regional and international markets. It is the fifth-largest financial centre in the United Kingdom outside London with more than 96,300 people employed in banking, finance, and insurance. The Co-operative Group, the world's largest consumer-owned business, is based in Manchester and is one of the city's biggest employers. Legal, accounting, management consultancy, and other professional and technical services exist in Manchester.

Manchester's commercial centre is in the centre of the city, adjacent to Piccadilly, focused on Mosley Street, Deansgate, King Street, and Piccadilly. Spinningfields is a £1.5 billion mixed-use development that is expanding the district west of Deansgate. The area is designed to hold office space, retail and catering facilities, and courts. Several high-profile tenants have moved in, and a Civil Justice Centre opened in October 2007.

Manchester is the commercial, educational and cultural focus for North West England, and in 2010 was ranked as the fourth biggest central retail area in the UK by sales. The city centre retail area contains shops from chain stores up to high-end boutiques such as Vivienne Westwood, Emporio Armani, DKNY, Harvey Nichols, Chanel, and Hermès.

7.1.10 - Map

Here is a map showing the whereabouts of Manchester within Britain.

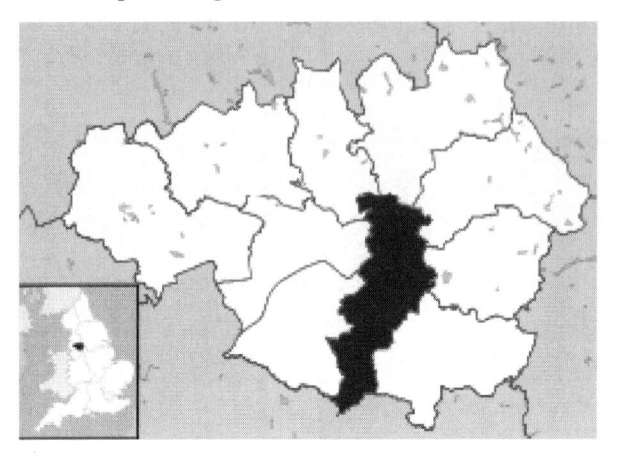

7.2 - Oldham

Oldham is a large town in Greater Manchester, England. It lies amid the Pennines on elevated ground between the rivers Irk and Medlock, 5.3 miles south-southeast of Rochdale, and 6.9 miles northeast of the city of Manchester. Oldham is surrounded by several smaller settlements which together form the Metropolitan Borough of Oldham, of which Oldham is the administrative centre.

Historically a part of Lancashire, and with little early history to speak of, Oldham rose to prominence during the 19th century as an international centre of textile manufacture. It was a boomtown of the Industrial Revolution, and among the first-ever industrialized towns, rapidly becoming "one of the most important centres of cotton and textile industries in England".At its zenith, it was the most productive cotton spinning mill town in the world, spinning more cotton than France and Germany combined.Oldham's textile industry began to fall into decline during the mid-20th century, and its last mill closed in 1998. It is part of Greater Manchester and is home to one of the oldest Bangladeshi communities in Britain.

Many of the immigrants who came to Burnley (like Mohammed Shamuz Miah) moved there to work in the local textile industry. The industry had grown up in the nineteenth century and Oldham was once the most productive cotton spinning mill town in the world. However, the cotton industry began to lose money in the 1970s and the last mill closed in 1998.

7.2.1 – History

The earliest known evidence of a human presence in what is now Oldham is attested by the discovery of Neolithic flint arrowheads and workings found at Werneth and Besom Hill, implying habitation 7–10,000 years ago. Evidence of later Roman and Celtic activity is confirmed by an ancient Roman road and Bronze Age archaeological relics found at various sites within the town.

Although Anglo-Saxons occupied territory around the area centuries earlier, Oldham as a permanent, named place of dwelling is believed to date from 865, when Danish invaders established a settlement called Aldehulme. From its founding in the 9th century until the Industrial Revolution, Oldham is believed to have been little more than a scattering of small and insignificant settlements spread across the moorland and dirt tracks that linked Manchester to York. Although not mentioned in the Domesday Book, Oldham does appear in legal documents from the Middle Ages, invariably recorded as territory under the control of minor ruling families and barons.

In the 13th century, Oldham was documented as a manor held from The Crown by a family surnamed Oldham, whose seat was at Werneth Hall. During the 1950s and 1960s, in an attempt to fill the shortfall of workers and revitalise local industries, citizens of the wider Commonwealth of Nations were encouraged to migrate to Oldham and other British towns. Many came from the Caribbean and Indian subcontinent and settled throughout the Oldham borough.

Bangladeshi migrants began to arrive in Oldham in large numbers in the 1960s and started to bring their families in the 1970s and 1980s. They settled close to each other for housing and shopping and to protect themselves from attacks by the National Front (a Far-Right racist political organisation that wanted all immigrants to leave Britain). The area they settled in was made up of six streets in Westwood. It became known as 'Bangla Para', and the area had a mosque and a community centre as well as shops selling Asian clothes and foods.

The population of Bangla Para is 99% Bengali. Most of the Bengali families in Oldham come from two main regions of Sylhet – Biswanath and Nabiganj, and these regions have the biggest influence on local politics and community organisations.

7.2.2 - Industrial Revolution

Cotton spinning and milling were introduced to Oldham when its first mill, Lees Hall, was built by William Clegg in about 1778, the beginning of a spiralling process of urbanization and socioeconomic transformation. Within a year, 11 other mills had been constructed, and by 1818 there were 19 – not a large number in comparison with other local settlements. Oldham's small local population was greatly increased by the mass migration of workers from outlying villages, resulting in a population increase from just over 12,000 in 1801 to 137,000 in 1901. The speed of this urban growth meant that Oldham, with little pre-industrial history to speak of, was effectively born as a factory town.

Oldham became the world's manufacturing centre for cotton spinning in the second half of the 19th century. In 1851, over 30% of Oldham's population was employed within the textile sector, compared to 5% across Great Britain. It overtook the major urban centres of Manchester and Bolton as the result of a mill building boom in the 1860s and 1870s, a period during which Oldham became the most productive cotton-spinning town in the world. In 1871 Oldham had more spindles than any country in the world except the United States, and in 1909, was spinning more cotton than France and Germany combined.

By 1911 there were 16.4 million spindles in Oldham, compared with a total of 58 million in the United Kingdom and 143.5 million in the world; in 1928, with the construction of the UK's largest textile factory, Oldham reached its manufacturing zenith. At its peak, there were over 360 mills, operating night and day;Oldham's townscape was dominated by distinctive rectangular brick-built mills. Oldham was hit hard by the Lancashire Cotton Famine of 1861–1865 when supplies of raw cotton from the United States were cut off.

Wholly reliant upon the textile industry, the cotton famine created chronic unemployment in the town. By 1863 a committee had been formed, and with aid from the central government, the land was purchased to employ local cotton workers to construct Alexandra Park, which opened on 28 August 1865. Said to have over-relied upon the textile sector,as the importation of cheaper foreign yarns grew during the 20th century, Oldham's economy declined into a depression, although it was not until 1964 that Oldham ceased to be the largest centre of cotton spinning.

Despite efforts to increase the efficiency and competitiveness of its production, the last cotton spun in the town was in 1998. In 1970 when Bangladeshi people came to the country they landed in Oldham. Oldham at that time was a mill area, cotton mills. Everyone worked there. 15 people would live in one house... One shift would sleep, when the other shift came home, the first shift would go to work and the others sleep in the same bed. That was how they lived; they would cook in turns. On their one day off, they would all go out. There was a cinema hall; they would go to the cinema. Indian films were shown.

Then the mills began to close...

When the Bengalis saw all the industries were closing, they thought about what else they could do. Bengalis are experts in new ideas - they found that there is one business that can be profitable and will run forever: the rice business... At that time, there were only two or three types of curry, not much. Now it is one of the biggest industries.

7.2.3 - Growth of Textile Trade

Much of Oldham's history is concerned with textile manufacture during the Industrial Revolution; it has been said that "if ever the Industrial Revolution placed a town firmly and squarely on the map of the world, that town is Oldham." Oldham's soils were too thin and poor to sustain crop growing, and so for decades before industrialisation the area was used for grazing sheep, which provided the raw material for a local woolen weaving trade.

By 1756, Oldham had emerged as centre of the hatting industry in England. The rough felt used in the production process is the origin of the term "Owdham Roughyed" a nickname for people from Oldham. It was not until the last quarter of the 18th century that Oldham changed from being a cottage industry township producing woollen garments via domestic manual labour, to a sprawling industrial metropolis of textile factories.

The climate, geology, and topography of Oldham were unrelenting constraints upon the social and economic activities of the human inhabitants. Located 700 feet (213 m) above sea level with no Major River or visible natural resources, Oldham had poor geographic attributes compared with other settlements for investors and their engineers.

As a result, Oldham played no part in the initial period of the Industrial Revolution, although it did later become seen as an obvious territory to industrialize because of its convenient position between the labour forces

144

of Manchester and southwest Yorkshire. Facilitated by its flourishing textile industry, Oldham developed extensive structural and mechanical engineering sectors during the 18th and 19th centuries.

The manufacture of spinning and weaving machinery in Oldham belongs to the last decade of the 19th century when it became a leading centre in the field of engineering. The Platt Brothers originated in nearby Dobcross village but moved to Oldham.

They were pioneers of cotton-spinning machinery, developing innovatory products which enabled the mass production of cotton yarn. Platt Brothers became the largest textile machine makers in the world, employing over 15,000 people in the 1890s, twice the number of their nearest rivals Dobson & Barlow in Bolton and Asa Lees on Greenacres Moor. They were keen investors in the local area and at one time, were supporting 42% of the population.

The centre of the company lay at the New Hartford Works in Werneth, a massive complex of buildings and internal railways on a site overlooking Manchester. The railway station which served this site later formed the basis of Oldham Werneth railway station, which together with the main building exists to this day. Platts gained prestigious awards from around the world and was heavily involved with local politics and civic pride in Oldham. John and James Platt were the largest subscribers for promoting Oldham from a township to a Borough, pledging £100 (more than double the next largest sum) in advance towards any expenses which may have been incurred by the Royal.

In 1854 John Platt was made the (fourth) Mayor of Oldham, an office he was to hold twice more in 1855–56 and 1861–62. John Platt was elected in 1865 to become Member of Parliament for Oldham, and was re-elected in 1868; he remained in office until he died in 1872. A bronze statue of Platt existed in the town centre for years, though was moved to Alexandra Park. There have been recommendations for it to be returned to the town centre.

7.2.4 - Population

The total population in Oldham is 103,544 (2001 Census), These two sources below show the population of Oldham and how it has changed dramatically throughout the years; also it shows the race of the certain population and how much they take up of Oldham.

The 2001 Census figures suggest that Bangladeshis are the third largest ethnic group in Oldham. They make up 4.5% of the population (about 9,900 people). It's thought that this will rise to over 10% (22,800 people) by 2021. The largest ethnic group is White British, and they make up 84.4% of the population. Oldham also has a large Pakistani population - 6.3%. Although Bangladeshis can be found in each of Oldham's 20 electoral wards, nearly half (49%) live in Coldhurst ward, with 11.9% in Werneth, 6.2% in Alexandra, and 6% in St Mary's Ward. Werneth, Alexandra, and St Mary's wards also have large Pakistani populations.

In Coldhurst, most Bangladeshis live in the Westwood, Glodwick, and Coppice areas. There was a lot of publicity about Glodwick in 2001 after the 'riots' in May. The 2009 census states that 218,800 people are living in Oldham and 10,300 of them are Bangladeshis.

Year	Population
1801	12.024
1811	16,690
1821	21,662
1831	32,381
1841	42,595
1851	52,820
1861	72,333
1871	82,629
1881	111,349
1891	131,492
1901	137,246
1911	147,483
1921	144, 983
1931	140,314
1939	120,511
1951	121,266
1961	115,346
1971	105,922
1981	107,830
1991	103,931
2001	103,544
2009	218,800
2011	

UK Census 2001	Oldham1	Oldham (Met. District)	England
Total population	103,5442	217,273	49,138,831
Foreign born	15%	8.2%	9.2%
White British	71%	86%	92%
Asian	27%	12%	4.6%
Black	0.9%	0.6%	2.3%
Christian	58%	73%	72%

Muslim	25%	11%	3.1%
Hindu	1.1%	0.1%	1.1%
No religion	8.3%	8.9%	15%
Over 65 years old	12%	14%	16%
Unemployed	5.5%	3.7%	3.3%

7.2.5 – Demography

According to data from the United Kingdom Census 2001, Oldham had a total resident population of 103,544, making it the 55th most populous settlement in England, and the 5th most populous settlement of the Greater Manchester Urban Area. This figure in conjunction with its area provides Oldham with a population density of 3,998 people per square mile.

The local population has been described as broadly "working class"; the middle classes tending to live in outlying settlements. Oldham, considered as a combination of the 2001 electoral wards of Alexandra, Coldhurst, Hollinwood, St. James, and St. Mary's, St. Paul's, Waterhead, and Werneth, has an average age of 33.5, and compared against the average demography of the United Kingdom, has a high level of people of South Asian heritage, particularly those with roots in Pakistan and Bangladesh. Due to the town's prevalence as an industrial centre and thus a hub for employment, Oldham attracted migrant workers throughout its history, including those from wider England, Scotland, Ireland, and Poland.

7.2.6 - Culture

Oldham, though lacking in leisure and cultural amenities, is historically notable for its theatrical culture. Once having a peak of six "fine" theatres in 1908, Oldham is home to the Oldham Coliseum Theatre and the Oldham Theatre Workshop, which have facilitated the early careers of notable actors and writers, including Eric Sykes, Bernard Cribbins, and Anne Kirkbride, daughter of acclaimed cartoonist Jack Kirkbride who worked for the Oldham Evening Chronicle.

Oldham Coliseum Theatre is one of Britain's last remaining repertories; Charlie Chaplin and Stan Laurel performed there in the early 20th century, and contemporary actors such as Ralph Fiennes and Minnie Driver, among others, have appeared more recently. In the nineteenth century, the circus was a popular entertainment in Oldham, with Pablo Fanque's circus, a regular visitor to town, filling a 3000-seat amphitheatre on Tommyfield in 1869.

Criticized for its lack of a cinema, there are plans to develop an "Oldham West End". Oldham has a thriving bar and nightclub culture which attracts a significant number of young people into the town centre. Oldham's "hard binge drinking culture" has been criticized however for conveying a negative regional image of the town. Most people are from Nabiganj and Biswanath. There are many people from these two districts. One mosque should be enough, but they say, 'Biswanath people come to this mosque, there is no-one from my region. Let us build a mosque for Nabiganj people.' That's how it is.

The Shahid Minar does not take much space. There is no other nation in the world that fought for their language. This was a unique movement. The Shahid Minar was finished at the end of 1996 and in '97 we opened it and presented flowers. Before that, there was no Shahid Minar in any foreign country outside of Bangladesh. Kamal Hossain told us that the celebrations of the Language Martyrs on 21 February (Ekushe) are a central meeting point for Bengalis from across the north of England:

People come from Manchester, Hyde, Burnley, Bradford, and even Birmingham to place flowers at the Shahid Minar from midnight... When people come, the road in front of the Shahid Minar is blocked. It is a huge gathering. The Shahid Minar is covered with flowers.Kamal eventuallymoved away from community politics because of growing divisions between people from different regions: Like the Bangladesh Association, the Council elections are dominated by regionalism - people from Nabiganj will vote for their candidate; Biswanath people vote for their candidate. The candidate with the most people from his region will win the election. Candidates from another region will not win.

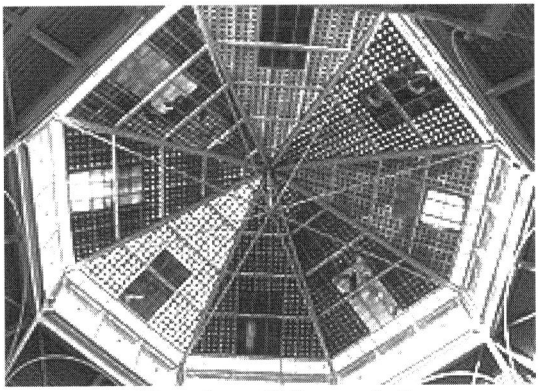

New photo Oldham spindle

7.2.7 - Social history

Oldham's social history, like that of other former enfranchised towns, is marked by politicized civil disturbances, as well as events related to the Luddite, Suffragette, and other Labour movements from the working classes. There has been a significant presence of "friendly societies". It has been put that the people of Oldham became radical in politics in the early part of the 19th century, and movements suspected of sedition found patronage in the town.

Oldham was frequently disturbed by bread and labour riots, facilitated by periods of scarcity and the disturbance of employment following the introduction of cotton-spinning machinery. On 20 April 1812, a "large crowd of riotous individuals" compelled local retailers to sell foods at a loss, whilst on the same day Luddites numbering in their thousands, many of whom were from Oldham, attacked a cotton mill in nearby Middleton.

On 16 August 1819, Oldham sent a contingent estimated at well above 10,000 to hear speakers in St Peter's Fields at Manchester discuss political reform. It was the largest contingent sent to Manchester. John Lees, a cotton operative and ex-soldier who had fought at Waterloo, was one of the fifteen victims of the Peterloo Massacre which followed. The 'Oldham inquest' which preceded the massacre was anxiously watched; the Court of King's Bench, however, decided that the proceedings were irregular, and the jury was discharged without giving a verdict.

Annie Kenney, born in nearby Springhead, and who worked in Oldham's cotton mills, was a notable of the Suffragette movement credited with sparking off suffragette militancy when she heckled Winston Churchill, and later (with Emmeline Pankhurst) the first Suffragist to be imprisoned. Oldham Women's Suffrage Society was established in 1910 with Margery Lees as president and quickly joined the Manchester and District Federation of the National Union of Women's Suffrage Societies. The Chartist and Co-operative movements had strong support in the town, whilst many Oldhamers protested against the emancipation of slaves. The Riot Act was read in 1852 on Election Day following a mass public brawl over the Reform Act, and irregularities with parliamentary candidate nominations.

For three days in late May 2001, Oldham became the centre of national and international media attention. Following high-profile race-related conflicts, and long-term underlying racial tensions between local White British and Asian communities, major riots broke out in the town. Occurring with particular intensity in the Glodwick area of the town, the Oldham riots were the worst racially motivated riots in the United Kingdom for fifteen years prior, briefly eclipsing the sectarian violence in Northern Ireland in the media.

At least 20 people were injured in the riots, including 15 police officers, and 37 people were arrested. Similar riots took place in other towns in northern England over the following days and weeks. The 2001 riots prompted governmental and independent inquiries, which collectively agreed on community relations improvements and considerable regeneration schemes for the town.

7.2.8 - Education

Almost every part of Oldham is served by a school of some kind, some with religious affiliations. According to the Office for Standards in Education, schools within the town perform at mixed levels. The Blue Coat School, which dates from 1834, is consistently Oldham's top-performing secondary school for 11- to 16-year-olds and has a sixth form college of further education for 16- to 18-year-olds on the same site.

Oldham produced someone who is considered to be one of the greatest benefactors of education for the nation, Hugh Oldham, who in 1504 was appointed as Bishop of Exeter, and later went on to found what is now Manchester Grammar School.

University Centre Oldham is a centre for higher education and a sister campus of the University of Huddersfield. It was opened in May 2005 by actor Patrick Stewart, the centre's Chancellor. The University Centre Oldham presented actress Shobna Gulati and artist, Brian Clarke (both born in Oldham) with an Honorary Doctorate of Letters at the Graduation Ceremony of November 2006, for their achievements and contributions to Oldham and its community.

7.2.9 - Economy

For years Oldham's economy was heavily dependent on the manufacturing industry, especially textiles and mechanical engineering. Since the deindustrialization of Oldham in the mid-20th century, these industries have been replaced by home shopping, publishing, and healthcare and food processing sectors, though factory-generated employment retains a significant presence. Many of the modern sectors are low-skill and low-wage.

Park Cake Bakeries, recently sold as part of a large shake-up by the Northern Foods Group, have a large food processing centre in Hathershaw, which employs more than 1,600 people. Over 90% of the cakes produced go to Marks & Spencer. Long existing as an industrial, Hollinwood is home to the Northern Counties Housing Association, and Mirror Colour Print Ltd; the printing division of the Trinity Mirror group, which prints and distributes 36 major newspapers, and employs 500 staff.

Oldham's town centre contains the highest concentration of retailing, cultural facilities, and employment in the Metropolitan Borough of Oldham. It has been extensively redeveloped during the last few decades, and its two shopping centres, Town Square and The Spindles, now provide one of the largest covered retail areas in Greater Manchester. The Spindles (named concerning textile spindles) is a modern shopping with over 40 retailers, banks, building societies, and catering outlets. It houses one of Europe's largest stained-glass roofs, created by local artist Brian Clarke in celebration of the music of one of Oldham's famous sons, composer, and conductor Sir William Walton.

Ferranti Technologies is an electronic, electromechanical, and Electrical Engineering Company based in Water head.

Several culinary and medical advances have been developed in Oldham. There are claims that Oldham was the birthplace of the first chip shop. The sometimes-disputed claim of trade in deep-fried chipped potatoes is said to have been started in around 1858–60 from an outlet owned by a John Lees, on what is the present site of Oldham's Tommy field Market.In 1900 Oldham had the highest concentration of chip shops in the country; one for every 400 people. Rag Pudding is a savoury dish said to be native to Oldham. Yates Wine Lodge was founded in Oldham by Peter and Simon Yates in 1884.

The tubular bandage was invented and developed in Oldham in 1961. That "vital contribution to advancing medical science" resulted from a collaboration between local firm Seton and a cotton manufacturer in the town.

Oldham was a business centre then. There were several textile mills. Many Bangladeshis worked there... At that time, Bengalis would only work and eat. They were mostly single people; they weren't family centred. Those were good times, we had strong friendships... From '68 to '69 more people came and after Liberation even more started coming.

Many people brought their families over after Liberation. Mohammed Aziz spoke of how the Bengali community had become more established: Earlier there was only one mosque in Oldham. It was difficult to provide a space for prayer. Society is expanding very fast. Earlier, there were 700 Bengalis in Oldham; now there are 15,000. So we decided to build a mosque in each area. Insha'Allah we now have 10 mosques in Oldham... We are trying to build a beautiful central mosque in Oldham.

The Bengali community in Oldham has always been very active, first as part of the Pakistan Welfare Association and, after Independence, the Bangladesh Welfare Association. The 1970s and 1980s saw the beginning of the Bangladesh Youth Association and Bangladesh Women's Association. They built Britain's first permanent Shahid Minar in 1997 and the Shapla Roundabout in 2000 (the Shapla flower is the national symbol of Bangladesh).

7.2.10 - Map

This is the map of Oldham, it is also showing where Oldham is situated within Great Britain.

7.3 – Rochdale

Rochdale is a large market town in Greater Manchester, England. It lies amongst the foothills of the Pennines on the River Roch, 5.3 miles (8.5 km) north-northwest of Oldham, and 9.8 miles (15.8 km) north-northeast of the city of Manchester. Rochdale is surrounded by several smaller settlements which together form the Metropolitan Borough of Rochdale, population 206,500. Rochdale is the largest settlement and administrative centre, with a total population of 95,796.

Historically a part of Lancashire, Rochdale's recorded history begins with an entry in the Domesday Book of 1086 under Recedham Manor. The ancient parish of Rochdale was a division of the hundreds of Salford and one of the largest ecclesiastical parishes in England comprising several townships. By 1251, Rochdale had become important enough to have been granted a Royal charter. Subsequently, Rochdale flourished into a centre of northern England's woollen trade, and by the early 18th century was described as "remarkable for many wealthy merchants".

Rochdale rose to prominence during the 19th century as a major mill town and centre for textile manufacture during the Industrial Revolution. It was a boomtown of the Industrial Revolution, and amongst the first ever industrialized towns. The Rochdale Canal—one of the major navigable broad canals of the United Kingdom—was a highway of commerce during this time used for the haulage of cotton, wool, and coal to and from the area. The socioeconomic change brought by the success of Rochdale's textile industry in the 19th century led to its rise to borough status and it remained a dominant settlement in its region.However, during the 20th century, Rochdale's spinning capacity declined towards an eventual halt.

Rochdale today is a predominantly residential town. Rochdale Town Hall—a Grade I listed building—dates from 1871 and is one of the United Kingdom's finest examples of Victorian Gothic revival architecture. Rochdale is the birthplace of the Co-operative Movement. The Rochdale Equitable Pioneers Society, founded in 1844, was the first modern cooperative; the Rochdale Principles are a set of ideals for cooperatives.

7.3.1 - History

Rochdale seems to be named from its position on the River Roch but is recorded as Recedham in the Domesday Book. The name is derived from Old English reced meaning "hall", and ham, a "homestead". Over time, the name changed to Rochdale and eventually Rochdale. During the time of the Danelaw, Rochdale was subjected to incursions by the Danes on the Saxons.

The castle that Castleton is named after, and of which no trace remains, was one of twelve Saxon forts possibly destroyed in frequent conflicts that occurred between the Saxons and Danes during the 10th and 11th centuries. Rochdale appears in the Domesday Book as Recedham.

At the time of the Norman Conquest, the manor was held by a Saxon thegn, Gamel. Before 1212 Henry II granted the manor to Roger de Lacy whose family retained it until it passed to the Dukes of Lancaster by marriage and then by 1399 to the. John Byron bought the manor in 1638 and it was sold by the poet, Lord Byron, in 1823, to the Dearden's, who holds the title.

Rochdale had no manor house but the "Orchard" built-in 1702 and acquired in 1745 by Simon Dearden was the home of the lords of the manor after 1823. It was described as "a red-brick building of no architectural distinction, on the north side of the river opposite the town hall" and sometimes referred to as the Manor House.

It was demolished in 1922. In medieval times, Rochdale was a market town, and weekly markets were held from 1250 when Edmund de Lacy obtained a grant for a market and an annual fair. The market was held outside the parish church where there was an "Orator's Corner". The manufacture of woollen cloth particularly baize, kerseys, and flannels were important from the reign of Henry VIII.

At this time the industry was rooted in the domestic system but towards the end of the 18th-century mills powered by water were built. Water power was replaced by steam power in the 19th century and coal mines, mostly drift mines, were opened where coal from the lower coal measures outcropped around the town. The Deardens who were lords of the manor were among the local coal owners.

7.3.2 - Industrial Revolution

The manufacture of woollen cloth particularly baize, kerseys, and flannels were important from the reign of Henry VIII. At this time the industry was rooted in the domestic system but towards the end of the 18th-century mills powered by water were built. Water power was replaced by steam power in the 19th century and coal mines, mostly drift mines, were opened where coal from the lower coal measures outcropped around the town.

The Deardens who were lords of the manor were among the local coal owners. By the mid-1800s the woollen trade was declining and the cotton trade which took advantage of technological developments in spinning and weaving growing in importance. Rochdale became one of the world's most productive cotton spinning towns when rose to prominence during the 19th century as a major mill town and centre for textile manufacture during the Industrial Revolution.

It was a boomtown of the Industrial Revolution, and amongst the first ever industrialized towns. By the end of the 19th century, there were woollen mills, silk manufacturers, bleachers, and dyers but cotton spinning and weaving were the dominant industries in Rochdale. The socioeconomic change brought by the success of Rochdale's textile industry in the 19th century led to its rise to borough status and it remained a dominant settlement in its region. However, during the 20th century Rochdale's spinning capacity declined towards an eventual halt.

The Rochdale Pioneers opened the first Cooperative shop in Toad Lane in 1844. The reformer and Member of Parliament, John Bright (1811–1889), was born in Rochdale and gained a reputation as a leader of political dissent and supporter of the Anti-Corn Law League.

7.3.3 - Growth of Textile Trade

By the mid-1800s the woollen trade was declining, and the cotton trade took advantage of technological developments in spinning and weaving growing in importance. Rochdale became one of the world's most productive cotton spinning towns when rose to prominence during the 19th century as a major mill town and centre for textile manufacture during the Industrial Revolution. It was a boomtown of the Industrial Revolution, and amongst the first ever industrialized towns.By the end of the 19th century, there were woollen mills, silk manufacturers, bleachers, and dyers but cotton spinning and weaving were the dominant industries in Rochdale.

The socioeconomic change brought by the success of Rochdale's textile industry in the 19th century led to its rise to borough status and it remained a dominant settlement in its region. However, during the 20th century, Rochdale's spinning capacity declined towards an eventual halt. The Rochdale Pioneers opened the first Cooperative shop in Toad Lane in 1844. The reformer and Member of Parliament, John Bright (1811–1889), was born in Rochdale and gained a reputation as a leader of political dissent and supporter of the Anti-Corn Law League.

7.3.4 - Population

The population within Rochdale is 95,765, below it shows the different races of people and how much they take up of the population. The 2009 Census states that 204,700 people are living there and 3,500 of them are Bangladeshis.

Rochdale compared			
2001 UK census	Rochdale	Rochdale MB	England
Total population	95,796	205,357	49,138,831
White	78.7%	88.6%	91%
Asian	19.9%	9.8%	4.6%
Black	0.3%	0.3%	2.3%
Christian	62.7%	72.1%	71.7%
Muslim	19.1%	9.4%	3.1%
No religion	10.4%	10.8%	14.6%

7.3.5 - Demography

As of the 2001 UK census, Rochdale had a population of 95,796. The 2001 population density was 11,186 inhabitants per square mile, with a 100 to 94.4 female-to-male ratio. Of those over 16 years old, 28.2% were single (never married), 44.0% were married, and 8.8% were divorced. Rochdale's 37,730 households included 30.4% one-person, 36.6% married couples living together, 8.4% were co-habiting couples, and 11.1% single parents with their children. Of those aged 16–74, 37.1% had no academic qualifications, similar to the figure for all of Rochdale, but higher than that of 28.9% in all of England. Rochdale has the highest number of Jobseeker's Allowance claimants in Greater Manchester, with 6.1 percent of its adult population claiming the benefit in early 2010.

7.3.6 - Education

Missing

7.3.7 – Map

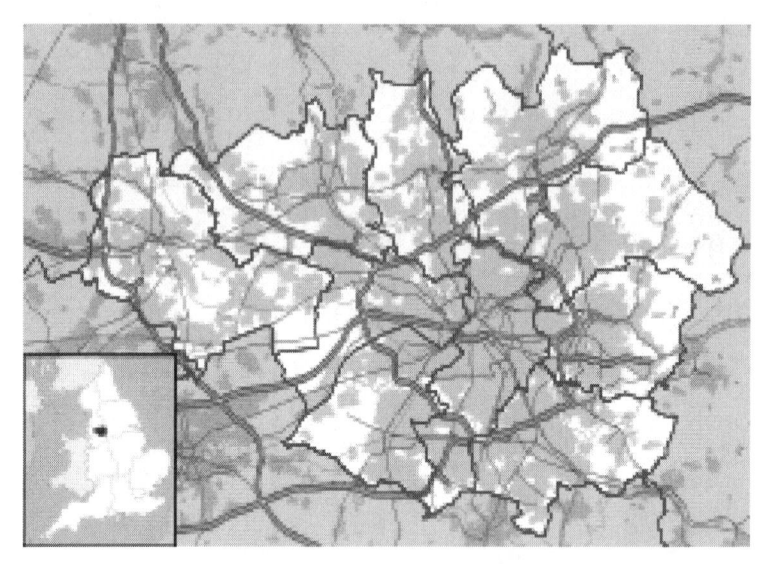

This map shows where Rochdale is situated within Great Britain.

7.4 – Tameside:

The Metropolitan Borough of Tameside is a metropolitan borough of Greater Manchester in North West England. It is named after the River Tame which flows through the borough and spans the towns of Ashton-under-

Lyne, Audenshaw, Denton, Droylsden, Dukinfield, Hyde, Mossley, and Stalybridge. Its western border is approximately 4 miles (6.4 km) east of Manchester city centre. It borders Derbyshire to the east, the Metropolitan Borough of Oldham to the north, the Metropolitan Borough of Stockport to the south, and the City of Manchester to the west. Tameside has a population of 214,400.

7.4.1 – History:

The history of the area extends back to the Stone Age. There are over 300 listed buildings in Tameside and three Scheduled Ancient Monuments, which include a castle of national importance. The settlements in Tameside were small townships centered on agriculture until the advent of the Industrial Revolution.

The towns of the borough grew and became involved in the cotton industry, which dominated the local economy. The current borough was created in 1974 as part of the provisions of the Local Government Act 1972. Since then, the area has been administered by Tameside Borough Council, which has been judged by the Audit to be "performing strongly".

The history of the area stretches back up to 10,000 years; there are 22 Mesolithic sites in Tameside, the oldest dating to around 8,000 BC; 21 of the 22 sites are in the hilly uplands in the northeast of the borough. Evidence of Neolithic and Age activity is more limited in the borough, although the Bronze Age Stalybridge Cairn is the most complete prehistoric funerary monument in the borough.

The people in the area changed from hunter-gatherers to farmers around 2500 BC–1500 BC due to climate change. Werneth Low is the most likely Iron Age farmstead site in the borough, probably dating to the late 1st millennium BC. Before the Roman conquest of Britain in the 1st century AD, the area was probably part of the territory of the Brigantes, the Celtic tribe controlling most of what is now North West England.

The area came under the control of the Roman Empire in the second half of the 1st century.

Roads through the area were established from Ardotalia fort in Derbyshire to Mamucium (Manchester) west of Tameside and Castle Shaw Roman fort in the north. Romano-British finds in the borough include a bog body in Ashton Moss, occupation sites at Werneth Low, Harridge Pike, Roe Cross, and Mottram. A 4th-century coin hoard was found in Denton and is one of only four hoards from the 4th century in the Mersey basin. A Byzantine coin from the 6th or 7th centuries, also found in Denton, indicates continued or renewed occupation once the Romans left Britain in the early 5th century.

Nico Ditch, an earthwork stretching from Stretford to Ashton-under-Lyne, is evidence of Anglo-Saxon activity in Tameside. It was probably dug between the 7th and 9th centuries and may have been used as a boundary between the kingdoms of Mercia and Northumbria. Further evidence of Anglo-Saxon era activity in Tameside comes from the derivation of settlement names from Old English such as -tun, meaning farmstead, and Leah meaning clearing.

According to the Domesday Survey of 1086, Tameside was divided into four manors, Tint istle, Hollingsworth, Werneth, and Mottram. The land east of the River Tame was in the Hundred of Hamestan in Cheshire and held by the Earl of Chester while to the west of the river was in the Hundred of Salford under Roger de Poitevin. These manors were divided to create further manors, so that by the 13th century. Most of them were owned by local families and remained in the hands of the same families until the 16th century. Manorialism continued as the main form of administration and governance until the mid-19th century.

7.4.2 - Industrial Revolution

The Industrial Revolution had a significant impact on Tameside; the area, whose main towns had previously been Ashton-under-Lyne and Mottram-in-Longdendale, was transformed from a collection of the rural, farming communities into mill towns. The towns of Ashton-under-Lyne, Dukinfield, Hyde, Mossley, and Stalybridge have been described as "amongst the most famous mills towns in the North West". With only a brief interruption for the Lancashire Cotton Famine of 1861 to 1865, factories producing and processing textiles were the main industry in Tameside from the late-18th century until the mid-20th century.

7.4.3 - Population

Although Tameside has only existed as a Metropolitan Borough since 1974, the table below details the population change – including the percentage change since the last census 10 years earlier – in the area since 1801 using figures from the towns, villages, and civil parishes that would later become constituent parts of Tameside. In the 2009 Census, the total population of Tameside was 215,400 and 3,000 of them are Bangladeshis.

Tameside Compared			
2001 UK Census	Tameside	Greater Manchester	England
Total population	213,043	2,514,757	49,138,831
White	94.6%	91.2%	90.9%
Asian	4.0%	5.6%	4.6%
Black	0.3%	1.2%	2.3%

Year	Population	% Change
1801	20,716	–
1811	27,219	+31.4
1821	45,440	+66.8
1831	64,044	+40.9
1841	103,928	+62.3
1851	120,183	+15.6
1861	129,346	+7.6
1871	138,509	+7.1
1881	147,672	+6.6
1891	158,343	+7.2
1901	175,877	+11.1
1911	195,353	+11.1
1921	192,764	-1.3
1931	190,210	-1.3
1941	198,492	+4.4
1951	207,137	+4.4
1961	213,973	+3.3
1971	221,067	+3.3
1981	217,050	-1.8
1991	219,769	+1.3
2001	213,043	-3.1
2009	215,400	+1.1

7.4.4 - Demography

As of the 2001 UK census, the Metropolitan Borough of Tameside had a total population of 213,043.Of the 89,981 households in Tameside, 35.7% were married couples living together, 31.0% were one-person households, 7.8% were co-habiting couples and 9.3% were lone parents, following a similar trend to the rest of England.

The population density was 2,065 /km2 and for every 100 females, there were 94.2 males. Of those aged 16–74 in Tameside, 35.2% had no academic qualifications, significantly higher than 28.9% in all of England. 4.8% of Tameside's residents were born outside the United Kingdom, significantly lower than the national average of 9.2%.The largest minority group was Asian, at 4.0% of the population.

In 1841, 8.5% of Tameside's population was middle class compared to 14% in England and Wales; this increased to 13.1% in 1931 (15% nationally) and 37.0% in 2001 (48% nationally). From 1841 to 1991, the working-class population of Tameside and across the country was in decline, falling steadily from 58.0% (36% nationally) to 22.8% in 1991 (21% nationally). It has since increased slightly, up to 32.9% (26% nationwide). The rest of the population was made up of clerical workers and skilled manual workers.

7.4.5 – Culture

"PORK Pies and Pasties" is Dukinfield artist Simeon Stafford's first retrospective exhibition. It reflects on Tameside, where he was brought up, and Cornwall, where he now lives. Simeon focuses on similar scenes to LS Lowry and Harry Rutherford but uses a wider palette and much thicker-layered paint to depict his old home, the street where he lived, and the people around him. His Cornish work is influenced by bright light, and while his Northern crowd scenes are from markets and fairs, the Cornish scenes show people frolicking in the sea and on the beaches.

7.4.6 - Social History

In 1964, Dukinfield Borough Council convened a meeting of neighbouring local authorities intending to formulate a policy of cross-authority social improvement for the districts in the Tame Valley. Following deindustrialization, the area had suffered "gross neglect" and had large areas of housing unsuitable for human habitation.

This joint enterprise comprised the nine districts that would become Tameside ten years later, plus the County Borough of Stockport. This collective agreed on creating "a linear park in the valley [of the River Tame] for the use of the townspeople and as a major recreational resource within the Manchester metropolis".

Tameside was created on 1 April 1974, by the Local Government Act 1972 as one of the ten metropolitan districts of Greater Manchester. It took over the local government functions of nine districts which were formerly in the administrative counties of Lancashire and Cheshire. In 1986 Tameside effectively became a unitary authority with the abolition of the Greater Manchester County Council.

A name for the metropolitan borough proved problematic. The Radcliffe-Maud Report had used the name Ashton-Hyde, but double-barrelled names were prohibited for the new districts.

Had Ashton-under-Lyne been a county borough, or had had a less common name, "it might have been chosen as the new name" for the new district. The eight other towns objected, adamant that "a new name should be found". Thirty suggestions were put forward, including Brigantia, Clarendon, Hartshead, Kay borough, Tame, Nine towns, and West Pennine, with Hartshead (about Hartshead Pike) being the most popular throughout most of the consultation period. However, the name Tameside (about the River Tame) won 15 votes to Harts's head's 10 in the final stage of voting.

The borough underwent a boundary review in 2002. The review altered the areas covered by some wards to ensure councillors represented roughly equal numbers. Between the 12th October 2006–08 and January 2007, a dispersal order was enforced in the Dukinfield and Newton Hyde areas of the borough. The move was designed to reduce anti-social behaviour. A representative of the Stalybridge police post said "Due to the serious nature of recent incidents in Dukinfield and Newton Hyde involving several confrontations between large groups of youths, the decision has been made to introduce a Dispersal Order".

7.4.7 - Education

Tameside council announced in 2007 a £180M plan to refurbish the borough's schools. The plan involves closing six schools and building six new ones. Overall the number of places available in schools will decrease as the number of school children is expected to decline. In 2007 Tameside was ranked 61st out of all the local education authorities in SATs performance – and 5th in Greater Manchester. Authorised absences from and unauthorised absences from Tameside secondary schools in 2006–07 were 6.0% and 0.4%, lower than the national average (7.8% and 1.4%).

In 2007, the Tameside LEA was ranked 100th out of 148 in the country – and 6th in Greater Manchester – based on the percentage of pupils attaining at least 5 A*-C grades at GCSE including maths and English (41.8% compared with the national average of 46.7%). In 2007, Audenshaw School was the most successful school in Tameside at both GCSE and A–level; 64% of the pupils gaining five or more GCSEs at A*-C grade including maths and English.
The secondary schools in Tameside are Alder Community High School, All Saints Catholic College, Astley Sports College, Audenshaw School, Copley

High School, Denton Community College, Droylsden Academy, Fairfield High School for Girls, Hyde Technology School, Longdendale Community Language College, Mossley Hollins High School, New Charter Academy, St Damian's RC Science College, St Thomas More RC High School and West Hill School

7.4.8 - Economy

The Ashton Arcades shopping centre opened in 1995. The centre covers 13,000 square meters (140,000 sq ft) on two floors with over 40 shops. In 2006, after failing twice to gain permission to develop a site in the neighbouring borough of Stockport, IKEA announced plans to build its first town centre-store in Ashton-under-Lyne.

The store is expected to create 500 new jobs as well as attract other businesses to the area. The store opened on 19 October 2006 and covers 27,500 square meters (296,000 sq ft) At the time of its creation, the store was the tallest in Britain. Life science industries have been identified as growth industries in Greater Manchester and are concentrated in Oldham and Tameside. Average house prices in Tameside are the 7th highest out of the ten metropolitan boroughs in Greater Manchester, 11.9% below the average for the county.

As of the 2001 UK census, Tameside had 152,313 residents aged 16 to 74. 2.0% of these people were students with jobs, 5.7% looking after home or family, 7.9% permanently sick or disabled, and 3.2% economically inactive for other reasons. In 2001, of 96,255 residents of Tameside in employment, the industry of employment was 21.7% manufacturing, 10.4% health and social work, 18.2% retail and wholesale, 10.2% property and business services, 7.2% construction, 6.8% transport and communications, 6.4% education, 5.3% public administration and defense, 4.2% finance, 4.0% hotels and restaurants, 0.9% energy and water supply, 0.5% agriculture, and 4.0% other. This was roughly in line with national figures, except for the proportion of jobs in agriculture which is less than half the national average, and property which was also below the national average. Manufacturing was 50% more than the national average.

Tameside Compared			
2001 UK Census	Tameside	North West England	England
Population of working age	152,313	4,839,669	35,532,091
Full time employment	43.5%	38.8%	40.8%
Part time employment	11.5%	11.9%	11.8%
Self employed	6.5%	7.1%	8.3%
Unemployed	3.3%	3.6%	3.3%
Retired	13.3%	14.3%	13.5%

7.4.9 - Map

This picture shows the exact position where Tameside is within Britain.

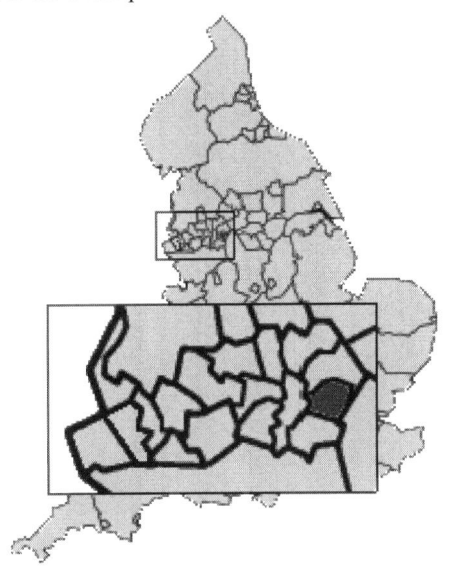

7.5 - Salford

Salford lies at the heart of the City of Salford, a metropolitan borough of Greater Manchester, in North West England. Salford is sited in a meander of the River Irwell, which forms its boundary with the city of Manchester to the east. Together with its neighbouring towns to the west, Salford forms the local government district of the City of Salford, which is administered from Swinton.

The former Borough of Salford, which included Broughton, Pendleton, and Kersal, was granted honorific city status in 1926; it has a resident population of 72,750 and occupies an area of 8.1 square miles (21 km2). The wider City of Salford district has a population of 219,200.

Historically a part of Lancashire, Salford's early history is marked by its status as a Royal caput and the judicial seat of the ancient hundred, to which it lent its name. It was granted a charter by Ranulf de Blondeville, 6th Earl of Chester, in about 1230, making Salford a free borough. During the early stages of its growth, Salford was of greater cultural and commercial importance than its neighbour Manchester, although most contemporary sources agree that since the Industrial Revolution of the late 18th and early 19th centuries that position has been reversed.

Salford became a major factory town and inland port during the 18th and 19th centuries. Cotton and silk spinning and weaving in local mills attracted an influx of families and provided Salford with a strong economy. Salford Docks was a principal dockyard of the Manchester Ship Canal.

By the end of the 19th century, Salford had an enlarged working-class community and suffered from chronic over. Industrial activities declined during the 20th century, however, causing a local economic depression. Salford subsequently became one of the contrasts, with regenerated inner-city areas like Salford Quays next to some of the most socially deprived and violent areas in England.

Salford has become a centre of higher education, home to the University of Salford, and has seen several firsts, including the world's first unconditionally free public library, and the first street in the world to be lit by gas, Chapel Street in 1806. Salford is set to become the headquarters of CBBC and BBC Sport in 2011.

7.5.1 - History

The earliest known evidence of human activity in what is now Salford is provided by the Neolithic flint arrowheads and workings discovered on Kersal Moor and the River Irwell, suggesting that the area was inhabited 7–10,000 years ago. The raw material for such tools was scarce and unsuitable for working, and as a result, they are not of the quality found elsewhere. Other finds include a Neolithic ax-hammer found near Mode Wheel, during the excavation of the Manchester Ship Canal in 1890, and a Bronze Age cremation urn during the construction of a road on the Broughton Hall estate in 1873.

The Brigantes were the major Celtic tribe in what is now Northern England. With a stronghold at the sandstone outcrop on which Manchester Cathedral now stands, opposite Salford's original centre, their territory extended across the fertile lowland by the River Irwell that is now Salford and Stretford. Following the Roman conquest of Britain, General Agricola ordered the construction of a Roman fort named Mamucium (Manchester) to protect the routes to Deva Victrix (Chester) and Eboracum (York) from the Brigantes. The fort was completed in AD 79, and for over 300 years the Pax Romana brought peace to the area. Both the main Roman road to the north, from Mamucium to Ribchester, and a second road to the west, ran through what is now Salford, but few Roman artifacts have been found in the area.

The withdrawal of the Romans in AD 410 left the inhabitants at the mercy of the Saxons. The Danes later conquered the area and absorbed what was left of the Brigantes. Angles settled in the region during the Early Middle Ages and gave the locality the name Sealhford, meaning "ford by the willows". According to the Anglo-Saxon Chronicle, Sealhford was part of the Kingdom of Northumbria until it was conquered in 923 by Edward the Elder.

Following the emergence of the United Kingdom of England, Salford became a caput or central manor within a broad rural area in part held by the Kings of England, including Edward the Confessor. The area between the rivers Mersey and Ribble was divided into six smaller districts, referred to as "wapentakes", or hundreds. The southeast district became known as the Hundred, a division of land administered from Salford for military and judicial purposes. It contained nine large parishes, smaller parts of two others, and the township of Aspull in the parish of Wigan.

After the defeat of Edward, the Confessor during the Norman conquest of England, William I granted the Hundreds of Salford to Roger the Poitevin, and in the Domesday Book of 1086, the Hundreds of Salford was recorded as covering an area of 350 square miles (906 km2) with a population of 35,000. Poitevin created the subordinate Manor of Manchester out of the hundred, which has since in local government been separate from Salford.

Poitevin forfeited the manor in 1102 when he was defeated in a failed rebellion attempt against Henry I. In around 1115, for their support during the rebellion, Henry I placed the Hundreds of Salford under the control of the Earldom of Lancaster, and it is from this exchange that the Hundreds of Salford became a royal manor. The Lord of the Manor was either the English monarch or a feudal landowner who administered the manor for the king. During the reign of Henry II, the Royal Manor of Salford passed to Ranulf de Gernon, 4th Earl of Chester.

Salford began to emerge as a small town early in the 13th century. In 1228, Henry III granted the caput of Salford the right to hold a market and an annual fair. The fairs were important to the town; a 17th-century order forced each burgess – a freeman of the borough – to attend, but the fairs were abolished during the 19th century.

The Earls of Chester aided the development of the caput, and in 1230 Ranulf de Blondeville, 6th Earl of Chester made Salford a burgage or free borough. The charter gave its burgesses certain commercial rights, privileges, and advantages over traders living outside Salford; one of the 26 clauses of the charter stated that no one could work in the Hundreds of Salford unless they also lived in the borough.

Salford's status as a burgage encouraged an influx of distinguished families, and by the Late Middle, Ages Salford was "rich in its manor houses", with over 30 within a 5-mile (8 km) radius of Ordsall. These included Ordsall Hall (owned by the Radclyffe family) and Broughton Hall, owned by the Earls of Derby.

During the Civil War of 1640–49, Salford supported the Royalist cause, in contrast to Manchester just across the Irwell which declared in favour of the Parliamentarians. Royalist forces mounted a siege of Manchester across what is now the site of Victoria Bridge, which although short-lived, "did little to improve relations between the two towns". A century later, in 1745, Salford was staunchly in support of Bonnie Prince Charlie, in his attempt to seize the Throne of England. He entered the town at the head of his army and was blessed by the Reverend John Clayton before leaving "in high spirits" to march on towards London; he returned to Salford in defeat just nine days later.

7.5.2 - Industrial Revolution

Salford has a history of textile processing that pre-dates the Industrial Revolution, and as an old town had been developing for about 700 years. Before the introduction of cotton, there was a considerable trade in woollen goods and fustians. Other industries prevalent at this time included clogging, cobbling, weaving and brewing. The changes to textile manufacture during the Industrial Revolution had a profound effect on both population and urbanisation, as well as the socioeconomic and cultural conditions of Salford.

Canal building provided a further stimulus for Salford's industrial development. The opening of the Bridgewater Canal in 1761 improved the transport of fuel and raw materials, reducing the price of coal by about 50%. The later Manchester, Bolton & Bury Canal (which terminated at Salford) brought more cheap coal from pits at Pendleton, Age croft Colliery, and beyond. By 1818 Manchester, Salford and Eccles had about 80 mills, but it was the completion of the Manchester Ship Canal in 1894 which triggered Salford's development as a major inland port.

Salford Docks, a major dockland on the Ship Canal 35 miles (56 km) east of the Irish Sea, brought employment to over 3,000 labourers. By 1914 the Port of Manchester, most of whose docks were in Salford, had become one of the largest port authorities in the world, handling 5% of the UK's imports and 4.4% of its exports. Commodities handled included cotton, grain, wool, textile machinery, and steam locomotives.

For centuries, textiles and related trades were the main sources of employment in the town. Bleaching was a widely distributed finishing trade in Salford, carried over from the earlier woollen industry. In the 18th century, before the introduction of chemical bleaching, bleaching fields were commonplace, some very close to the town. In 1773 there were 25 bleachers around Salford, most to the west of the township.

Printing was another source of trade; the earliest recorded in the region was a clique printer in the Manchester Parish Register of 1763. These industries became more important as Salford faced increasing competition from the nearby towns of Bolton and Oldham. As its cotton spinning industries faltered its economy turned increasingly to other textiles and the finishing trades, including rexine and silk dyeing, and fulling and bleaching, at a string of works in Salford.

Both Karl Marx and Friedrich Engels spent time in Salford, studying the plight of the British working class. In The Condition of the Working Class in England in 1844, Engels described Salford as "really one large working-class quarter ... [a] very unhealthy, dirty, and dilapidated district which, while other industries were almost always textile-related is situated opposite the 'Old Church' of Manchester".

Salford developed several civic institutions; in 1806, Chapel Street became the first street in the world to be lit by gas (supplied by Phillips and Lee's cotton mill). In 1850, under the terms of the Museums, the municipal borough council established the Royal Museum and Public Library, said to have been the first unconditionally free public library in England, preceding the Public Libraries Act 1850.

The effect on Salford of the Industrial Revolution has been described as "phenomenal". The area expanded from a small market town into a major industrial metropolis; factories replaced cottage industries, and the population rose from 12,000 in 1812 to 70,244 within 30 years.

By the end of the 19th century, it had increased to 220,000. Large-scale buildings of low-quality Victorian terraced housing did not stop overcrowding, which itself lead to chronic social deprivation. The density of housing was as high as 80 homes per acre. Private roads were built for the use of the middle classes moving to the outskirts of Salford. The entrances to such roads, which included Elleray Road in Irlams o' Th' Height, were often gated and patrolled.

7.5.3 - Growth of Textile Trade

The well-established textile processing and trading infrastructure, and the ready supply of water from the River Irwell and its tributaries, attracted entrepreneurs who built cotton mills along the banks of the river in Pendleton and Ordsall. Although Salford followed a similar pattern of industrial development to Manchester, most businesses preferred to build their premises on the Manchester side of the Irwell, and consequently, Salford did not develop as a commercial centre in the same way as its neighbour.

Many of these earlier mills had been based on Arkwright-type designs. These relied on strong falls of water, but Salford is on a meander of the Irwell with only a slight gradient and thus mills tended to be built upstream, at Kersal and Pendleton. With the introduction of the steam engine in the late 18th century, however, merchants began to construct mills closer to the centres of Salford and Manchester, where supplies of labour and coal were more readily available (the first steam-powered mill was built in Manchester in 1780).

One of the first factories to be built was Philip's and Lee's Twist Mill in Salford, completed in 1801, the second iron-framed multi-story building to be erected in Britain. The large Salford Engine Twist Company mill was built to the west of Salford, between Chapel Street and the Irwell, and in 1806 was the first large cotton mill to use gaslighting. It was however outnumbered by the numerous smaller factories and mills throughout the area, including Nathan Gough's steam-driven mule spinning mill, near Oldfield Road, where a serious accident occurred on 13 October 1824.

7.5.4 - Population

Within Salford, there are 72,750 people (Census 2001). The 2009 Census states that 225,100 people are living there and that 900 of them are from Bangladesh.

Year	1901	1911	1921	1931	1939	1951	1961	1971	1981	1991	2001	2009
Population	162,452	172,998	234,045	223,438	166,386	178,194	155,090	131,006	98,343	79,755	72,750	225,100

Salford compared			
2001 UK census	Salford	City of Salford	England
Total population	72,750	210,145	49,138,831
White	93.9%	96.1%	91%
Asian	1.9%	1.4%	4.6%
Black	1.2%	1.2%	2.3%

Both these charts show the population of people in the UK (Salford) and it also shows the Demography.

7.5.5 - Demography

As of the 2001 UK census, Salford had a population of 72,750. The 2001 population density was 9,151 per mi^2 (3,533 per km^2), with a 100 to 98.4 female-to-male ratio. Of those over 16 years of age, 44.0% were single (never married) and 36.7% were married. Salford's 32,576 households included 44.1% one-person, 22.0% married couples living together, 7.6% were co-habiting couples, and 13.3% single parents with their children.Of those aged 16–74, 37.3% had no academic qualifications, similar to that of 35.5% in all of the City of Salford but significantly higher than 28.9% in all of England. 15.9% of Salford's residents aged 16–74 had an educational qualification such as first degree, higher degree, qualified teacher status, qualified medical doctor, qualified dentist, qualified nurse, midwife, health visitor, etc. compared to 20% nationwide.

As a result of 19th-century industrialization, Salford has had "a special place in the history of the British working class"; together with Manchester it had the world's "first fully formed industrial working class". Salford has not, in general, attracted the same minority ethnic and cosmopolitan communities as in other parts of Greater Manchester, although it did attract significant numbers of Irish in the mid-19th century. Many migrated to Salford because of the Great Hunger in Ireland combined with Salford's reputation as a hub for employment in its factories and docks.In 1848, Salford Roman Catholic Cathedral opened, reflecting the large Irish-born community in Salford at that time.

In the decades following the Second World War Salford experienced significant population decline, as residents followed employment opportunities to other locations in Greater Manchester, taking advantage of a greater choice in the type and location of housing.

7.5.6 - Culture

Salford Museum and Art Gallery opened in November 1850 as the Royal Museum and Public Library. It was built on the site of Lark Hill estate and Mansion, which was purchased by public subscription. The park was named Peel Park after Robert Peel who contributed to the subscription fund. The library was the first unconditionally free public library in the country.

Harold Brighouse's play Hobson's choice takes place in the Salford of 1880, and the 1954 film version was shot in the town. Walter Greenwood's 1933 novel Love on the Dole was set in a fictional area known as Hanky Park, said in the novel to be near Salford, but in reality based on Salford itself.

A more modern fictional setting influenced by the area is Coronation Street's Weatherfield. The Salford of the 1970s was the setting for the BAFTA award-winning East is east. Salford was featured in the second series of Channel 4's programme The Secret Millionaire, screened in 2007.

The folk song "Dirty Old Town", written by native Ewan MacColl, is the origin of Salford's nickname. Local band Doves released a song on their 2005 album Some Cities called "Shadows of Salford". One of the most famous photographs of the band The Smiths shows them standing outside the Salford Lads Club, and was featured in the artwork for their album The Queen Is Dead. The videos for the Timberlands song "The Way I Are", and the Justin Timberlake song "Lovestoned" were filmed in Salford.

7.5.7 - Education

Despite the rapid progress made during the Industrial Revolution, by 1851 education in Salford was judged "inadequate to the wants of the population", and for those children who did get schooling "order and cleanliness were little regarded ... [they] were, for the most part, crowded in close and dirty rooms".

Salford has thirty-two primary schools and five secondary schools. Until recently there were three main 6th form and FE colleges: Pendleton College, Eccles College, and Salford College. They merged to create Salford City College in January 2009.

The University of Salford, a plate glass university, is one of four in Greater Manchester. It has its origins in the former Royal Technical College, which was granted the status of a College of Advanced Technology (CAT), on 2 November 1956. In November 1963, the Robbins Report recommended that the CATs should become technological universities; and on 4 April 1967, a Charter was established creating the University of Salford. The university is undergoing £150M of redevelopment through investment in new facilities, including a £10M law school and a £22M building for health and social care, which were opened in 2006.

The University of Salford has over 19,000 students and was ranked 81st in the UK by The Times newspaper. In 2007, the university received nearly 17,000 applications for 3,660 places, and the drop-out rate from the university was 25%. Of the students graduating, 50% gained first-class or 2:1 degree, below the national average of about 55%. The level of student satisfaction in the 2009 survey ranged from 62% to 94%, depending on the subject.

7.5.8 - Economy

For decades Salford's economy was heavily dependent on the manufacturing industry, especially textiles and engineering. Since the Second World War, however, Salford has experienced decades of growing unemployment as these sectors diminished and new sectors chose to locate in out-of-town locations with better transport links.

Between 1965 and 1991 the city lost over 49,000 jobs or more than 32% of its employment base. Several factors contributed to this decline, not least changes in the national and international economies, the introduction of new technology, and the concentration of investment in London and Southeast England. The biggest job losses were experienced in Salford's traditional industries and although the service sector expanded during this period, it was unable to compensate for the decline in manufacturing.

The inner city's main shopping area is Salford Shopping City, Pendleton – colloquially referred to as "Salford Precinct" – close to the University of Salford. However, this area suffers from extreme deprivation and is dominated by the central business district that is Manchester city centre. This is planned to change in the next few years with the implementation of the Pendleton Area Action Plan and the development of the pedestrianised and boulevard A6 corridor. Salford Quays has been shortlisted as the new possible city centre by 2020.

The Lowry Hotel, the first five-star hotel to be built in Greater Manchester, is on the Salford side of the River Irwell. Salford is credited as the birthplace of the Bush Roller Chain. Hans Renold, a Swiss-born engineer, came to Salford in the late 19th century. In 1879 he purchased a small textile-chain-making business in Ordsall from James Slater and founded the Hans Renold Company, what is now Renold, a firm that still produces chains.

Renold invented the bush roller chain shortly after and began producing it. It is the type of chain most commonly used for transmission of mechanical power on bicycles, motorbikes, to industrial and agricultural machinery to uses as varied as rollercoasters and escalators.

According to the 2001 UK census, the industry of employment of Salford's residents aged 16–74 was 18.0% retail and wholesale, 14.4% property and business services, 12.3% manufacturing, 11.7% health and social work, 8.6% education, 7.3% transport and communications, 6.8% hotels and restaurants, 5.8% construction, 4.4% finance, 4.2% public administration, 0.6% energy and water supply, 0.3% agriculture, 0.1% mining, and 5.7% other.

Compared with national figures, Salford had a relatively low percentage of residents working in agriculture. The census recorded the economic activity of residents aged 16–74, 4.4% students were with jobs, 9.1% students without jobs, 6.3% looking after home or family, 11.2% permanently sick or disabled, and 4.8% economically inactive for other reasons. The proportion of students economically active in Salford was higher than the City of Salford and England averages (3.0% and 2.6% respectively); the same is true for economically inactive students (5.1% in the City of Salford and 4.7% in England). The rest of the figures were roughly in line with national trends.

Salford compared			
2001 UK Census	Salford	City of Salford	England
Population of working age	52,992	216,103	35,532,091
Full time employment	34.0%	39.3%	40.8%
Part time employment	9.6%	10.6%	11.8%
Self employed	4.6%	5.4%	8.3%
Unemployed	4.3%	3.8%	3.3%
Retired	12.0%	13.5%	13.5%

7.5.9 - Map

This map shows exactly where Salford is within Britain.

7.6 – Conclusion

Bangladeshis are one of the largest immigrant communities in the United Kingdom. Significant numbers of ethnic Bengalis arrived as early as the 17th century, including Sylhetis, who mostly arrived as lascar seamen working on ships. Following the founding of Bangladesh in 1971, large immigration to Britain took place during the 1970s, leading to the establishment of a British Bangladeshi community.

Bangladeshis were encouraged to move to Britain during that decade because of changes in immigration laws, natural disasters such as the Bhola cyclone, the Bangladesh Liberation War against Pakistan, and the desire to escape poverty, and the perception of a better living led Sylheti men to bring their families. They initially experienced high rates of racial attacks and unemployment but have since integrated into British society over the last several decades.

Bibliography

Bangladeshi Restaurant Curries, Piatkus, London — ISBN 0749916184 (1996)

Curries - Master chef Series, Orion, London — ISBN 0297836420 (1996)

Curry, Human & Rousseau, South Africa — ISBN 0798131934 (1993)

Kerrie, in Afrikaans, Human & Rousseau, South Africa — ISBN 0798128143 (1993)

Petit Plats Curry, French edition, Hachette Marabout, Paris — ISBN 2501033086 (2000)

2009 Cobra Good Curry Guide, John Blake Publishing, London — ISBN 1-84454-311-0

References

Alam - 1988

Ali – 1996

Ahmed Kaufman & Naim – 1996

Bangladesh Bureau of Statistics – Government of the People's Republic of Bangladeh

Badawi, Zaki (1995): 'Muslim justice in a secular state' In: Michael King (ed): God's law verses state law: The construction of an Islamic identity in Western Europe. London: Grey Seal, pp. 73-80.

Ballard, Roger (ed.) (1994): Desh pardesh: the South Asian presence in Britain. London: Hurst & Co.

Ballard, Roger (1996): 'Panth kismet dharm te quam: continuity and change in four dimensions of Punjabi religion'. In: Pritam Singh and Shinder S. Thandi (eds.): Globalisation and the region. Explorations in Panjabi identity. Coventry: Association for Punjabi Studies, pp. 7-38.

Ballard, Roger (2001a): 'Popular Islam in northern Pakistan and its reconstruction in Britain'. Paper presented at the International Workshop on Islamic Mysticism in the West, Buxton, Derbyshire, 22-24 July 2001, also at www.casas.org.uk.

Ballard, Roger (2001b): 'The impact of kinship on the economic dynamics of transnational networks: reflections on some South Asian developments'. Paper presented at Workshop on Transnational Migration, Princeton University, 29 June – 1 July 2001, also at www.casas.org.uk and at www.transcomm.ox.ac.uk.

Ballard, Roger (n.d.): 'Common law and uncommon sense: the assessment of reasonable behavior in a plural society', at www.casas.org.uk.

Chiba, Masaji (1986): Asian indigenous law in interaction with received law. London and New York: Kegan Paul International.

Carey & Shukur – 1985

Carroll – 1997

Chiefly, Menski - 1993

Drabu, Khurshid and Stephen Bowen (1989): Mandatory Visas. Visiting the UK from Bangladesh, India, Pakistan, Ghana and Nigeria. London: Commission for Racial Equality.

Eade, John, Tim Vamplew and Ceri Peach (1996): 'The Bangladeshis: the encapsulated community'. In: Ceri Peach (ed.): Ethnicity in the 1991 Census. Volume two. The Ethnic minority populations of Great Britain. London: HMSO, pp. 150-160.

Fransman, Laurie (1986): 'Family settlement cases: a denial of statutory rights'. In: Vol. 1, No. 1 Immigration and Nationality Law and Practice, pp. 5-15.

Fransman, Laurie (1989): British nationality law. London: Fourmat.

Gardner, Katy (1993): 'Desh-bidesh: Sylheti images of home and away'. In: Vol. 28, No. 1 Man, pp. 1-15.

Gardner, Katy (1995): Global migrants, local lives. Oxford: Clarendon.

Gardner, Katy and Abdus Shukur (1994): '"I'm Bengali, I'm Asian, and I'm living here": the changing identity of British Bengalis'. In: Roger Ballard (ed.) (1994): Desh pardesh: the South Asian presence in Britain. London: Hurst & Co., pp. 142-164.

Gillespie, Jim (1992): 'Maintenance and accommodation and the immigration rules: recent developments'. In: Vol. 6, No. 3 Immigration and Nationality Law and Practice, pp. 97-100.

Glenn, H. Patrick (2000): Legal systems of the world. Oxford: Oxford University Press.

Griffiths, John (1986): 'What is legal pluralism?' In: No. 24 Journal of Legal Pluralism and Unofficial Law, pp. 1-55.

Haddad - 1986

Hooker, M. B. (1975): Legal pluralism. Oxford: Clarendon Press.

Hussein, Raza and Duran Seddon (1996): 'Recourse to public funds and indirect reliance'. In: Vol. 10, No. 2 Immigration and Nationality Law and Practice, pp. 50-53.

Joint Council for the Welfare of Immigrants (1987): Out of sight. The new visit visa system overseas. London: JCWI.

Jones, Richard and Gnanapala Welhengama (2000): Ethnic minorities in English law. London: Group for Ethnic Minority Studies, SOAS and Stoke on Trent: Trentham.

Juss, Satvinder S. (1997): Discretion and deviation in the administration of immigration control. London: Sweet and Maxwell.

Kenny - 2002

Mayss, Abla (2000): 'Recognition of foreign divorces: unwarrantable ethnocentrism'. In: John Murphy (ed.): Ethnic minorities, their families and the law. Oxford, UK and Protland, Oregon: Hart, pp. 51-70.

McKee, Richard (1995): 'A burden on the taxpayer? Some developments in the role of 'public funds' in immigration law'. In: Vol. 9, No. 1 Immigration and Nationality Law and Practice, pp. 29-31.

Menski, Werner (1988): 'Uniformity of laws in India and England'. In: Vol. VII, No. 11 Journal of Law and Society (Peshawar), pp. 11-26.

Menski, Werner (1993): 'Asians in Britain and the question of adaptation to a new legal order: Asian laws in Britain?' In: M Israel and N K Wagle (eds.): Ethnicity, identity, migration: the South Asian context. Toronto: Centre for South Asian Studies, University of Toronto, pp. 238-268.

Menski, Werner (1994): 'Family migration and the new immigration rules'. In: Vol. 8, No. 4 Immigration and Nationality Law and Practice, pp. 112-124.

Menski, Werner F. (1997): 'South Asian Muslim law today: an overview'. In: Vol. 9, No. 1 Sharqiyyat, pp. 16-36.

Menski, Werner F. (2000): Comparative law in a global context: the legal systems of Asia and Africa. London: Platinium.

Menski, Werner F. (2001): 'Muslim law in Britain'. In: No. 62 Journal of Asian and African Studies, pp. 127-163.

Menski, Werner and Tahmina Rahman (1988): 'Hindus and the law in Bangladesh'. In: Vol. 8, No. 2 South Asia Research, pp. 111-131.

Mistry, Hiren Bhana (1999): Diaspora and sadacara: the legal reconstruction of Hinduism in ancient and classical India. MA dissertation, School of Oriental and African, London.

Modood, Tariq and Richard Berthoud (eds.): Ethnic minorities in Britain. London: PSI.

Monsoor, Taslima (1999): From patriarchy to gender equity. Family law and its impact on women in Bangladesh. Dhaka: The University Press Ltd. Nielsen,

Jorgen (1988): 'Muslims in Britain and local authority responses. In: T. Gerholm and Y. Lithman (eds.): The new Islamic presence in Western Europe. London: Mansell, pp. 53-77.

Naim- 2003

Nielsen, Jorgen (1992): 'Islam, Muslims, and British local and central government'. Paper presented at conference on Muslims in Europe, Turin, 4-5 May 1992.

Peach - 1990

Pearl, David (1986): Family law and the immigrant communities. Bristol: Jordan & Sons.

Pearl, David and Werner Menski (1998): Muslim family law. London: Sweet and Maxwell.

Poulter, Sebastian (1986): English law and ethnic minority customs. London: Butterworths.

Poulter, Sebastian (1990): 'The claim to a separate Islamic system of personal law for British Muslims'. In: Chibli Mallat and Jane Connors (eds.): Islamic family law. London: Graham and Trotman, pp. 147-166.

Poulter, Sebastian (1998): Ethnicity, law, and human rights. Oxford: Clarendon Press.

Sachdeva, Sanjiv (1993): The primary purpose rule in British immigration law. Stoke on Trent: Trentham.

Shah, Prakash (1994): 'Legal pluralism – British law and possibilities with Muslim ethnic minorities. In: Nos. 66/67 Retfærd, pp. 18-33.

Shah, Prakash (2002): 'Attitudes to polygamy in English law'. Unpublished paper.

Shah-Kazemi, Sonia-Nurin (2001): Untying the knot: Muslim women, divorce and the shariah. London: Nuffield Foundation.

Samad & Eade – 2002

Salazar – 2001

Sek Pye Lim - 2001

Wray, Helena and Mahmud Quayum [1999]: 'Entry clearance application for spouses where sponsor is on benefits. In: 13(4) I&NL&P 133-135.

Willet - 1998

Wrench & Qureshi - 1996

Yilmaz, Ihsan (1999): Dynamic legal pluralism and the reconstruction of unofficial Muslim laws in England, Turkey, and Pakistan. PhD Thesis, London: School of Oriental and African Studies.

Yilmaz, Ihsan (2000): 'Muslim law in Britain: reflections in the socio-legal sphere and differential legal treatment'. In: Vol. 21, No. 2 Journal of Muslim Minority Affairs, pp. 353-360.

Yilmaz, Ihsan (2001): 'Law as chameleon: the question of incorporation of Muslim personal law into the English law'. In: Vol. 21, No. 2 Journal of Muslim Minority Affairs, pp. 297-308.

Source of Information from Internet:

[1] Wikipedia
http://en.wikipedia.org/wiki/list of countries and outlying territories by total area

[2] Bangladesh Bureau of statistics – Population & Housing Census 2011 Preliminary Results July 2011

[3] The Economist Intelligence Unit
http://country.eiu.com/article.aspx?articleid=218456206&Country=Banglades h&topic=Summary&subtopic=Fact+sheet&subsubtopic=Factsheet

[4] Greater London Authority Intelligence Update – 20th June 2010 (issued 30th June 2011)
http://www.london.gov.uk/sites/default/files/Update%2011-2011%20mid 2010%20population%20estimates.pdf

[5] CIA World Fact Book
http://www.cia.gov/library/publications/the-world-factbook/geos/bg.html

[6] BBC
http://www.bbc.co.uk/news/world-south-asia-14967857

[7] The Economist
http://www.economist.com/blogs/dailychart/2011/01/comparing us states countries

[8] The World Bank Data Bank
http://search.worldbank.org/all?gterm=bangladesh

[9] Population Division of the department of Economic and Social Affairs of the United Nations Secretariat, World Population Prospects: The 2010 Revision

[10] Human Development Reports – United Nations Development Program
http://hdr.undp.org/en/statistics/

[11] Transparency International – Corruption Perceptions Index 2010
http://www.transparency.org/policy research/surveys indices/cpi/2010/results

[12]https://en.wikipedia.org/wiki/Afshan_Azad[9.8.2021]

[13]https://twitter.com/mumzystranger/status/1007557040435335168[9.8.2021]

[14]https://twitter.com/SyedAhmed/status/1064564559128772608/photo/1[9.8.2021]

If you liked this book,
then check out the catalogue!

MAPublisher Catalogue

ISBN/Titles /Image/Author	ISBN/Titles /Image/Author	ISBN/Titles /Image/Author	ISBN/Titles /Image/Author
978-1-910499-00-9 Father to child By Mayar Akash	978-1-910499-08-5 HSJ Lakri Tura By Mayar Akash	978-1-910499-26-9 Colouring 1-10 By MAPublisher	978-1-910499-18-4 Basic Numbers 1-10 By MAPublisher
978-1-910499-16-0 River of Life By Mayar Akash	978-1-910499-09-2 HSJ Gilaf Procession By Mayar Akash	978-1-910499-27-6 Activity Numbers 1-10 By MAPublisher	978-1-910499-19-1 Number 1-100 By MAPublisher
978-1-910499-39-9 Eyewithin By Mayar Akash	978-1-910499-03-0 HSJ Mazar Sharif By Mayar Akash	978-1-910499-28-3 Activity Colouring Alphabets By MAPublisher	978-1-910499-20-7 Vowels By MAPublisher
978-1-910499-32-0 WG Survivor By Mayar Akash	978-1-910499-06-1 Hazrat Shahjalal By Mayar Akash	978-1-910499-68-9 The Adventures of Sylheti mazars By Mayar Akash	978-1-910499-21-4 Alphabet Consonants By MAPublisher
978-1-910499-66-5 Yesteryears By Mayar Akash	978-1-910499-07-8 HSJ Urus By Mayar Akash	978-1-910499-38-2 Bite Size Islam: 99 Names of Allah By Mayar Akash	978-1-910499-22-1 Vowels & Short By MAPublisher

189

ISBN/Titles /Image/Author	ISBN/Titles /Image/Author	ISBN/Titles /Image/Author	ISBN/Titles /Image/Author
978-1-910499-15-3 Anthology One By Penny Authors	978-1-910499-36-8 Delirious By Liam Newton	978-1-910499-52-8 Lit From Within By Ruth Lewarne	978-1-910499-57-3 The Vampire of the Resistance By Ruth Lewarne
978-1-910499-17-7 Anthology Two By Penny Authors	978-1-910499-54-2 Book of Lived v6 Penny Authors	978-1-910499-49-8 Cry for Help By B. M. Gandhi	978-1-910499-55-9 Riversolde By Meriyon
978-1-910499-29-0 Book of Lived v3 By Penny Authors	978-1-910499-37-5 When You Look Back By Rashma Mehta	978-1-910499-14-6 The Halloweeen Poem by Zainab Khan	978-1-910499-70-2 Smiley & The Acorn By Roger Underwood
978-1-910499-351 V4 Book of Lived By Penny Authors	978-1-910499-37-5 My Dream World By Rashma Mehta	978-1-910499-69-6 Consciousness By Mustak Mustafa	978-1-910499-40-5 World's First University By Giasuddin Ahmed
978-1-910499-50-4 Book of Lived v5 By Penny Authors	978-1-910499-53-5 Angel Eyez By Rashma Mehta	978-1-910499-73-3 Book of Lived v7 By Penny Authors	978-1-910499-56-6 The Warrior Queen By Giasuddin Ahmed

All books are available on-line, Google the titles and they will take you to the sites where you can acquire copies.

https://www.waterstones.com/author/mayar-akash/1973183 [3.11.21]

ISBN/Titles /Image/Author	ISBN/Titles /Image/Author	ISBN/Titles /Image/Author	ISBN/Titles /Image/Author
978-1-910499-58-0 EEP:Tower Hamlets, Random, One Mayar Akash	978-1-910499-60-3 EEP:Tower Hamlets, Random, Two By Mayar Akash	978-1-910499-05-4 Tide of Change By Mayar Akash	978-1-910499-51-1 Brick & Mortar By Mayar Akash
978-1-910499-61-0 Grenfell Tower By Mayar Akash	978-1-910499-63-4 EEP: Power Houses, Clove Crescent By Mayar Akash	978-1-910499-71-9 Altab Ali Murder By Mayar Akash	978-1-910499-31-3 Pathfinders By Mayar Akash
978-1-910499-62-7 EEP: Community Service 1992-1993 By Mayar Akash	978-1-910499-64-1 EEP:Bancroft Estate By Mayar Akash	978-1-910499-11-5 Re-Awakening By Mayar Akash	978-1-910499-13-9 Chronicle of Sylhetis of UK By Mayar Akash
978-1-910499-59-7 EEP:Brick Lane, Spitalfields By Mayar Akash	978-1-910499-72-6 25th Anniversary of Bangladesh By Mayar Akash	978-1-910499-12-2 Young Voice Mayar Akash	978-1-910499-42-9 Bangladeshi Fishes By Mayar Akash
978-1-910499-65-8 PYO Polish Exchange 1992 By Mayar Akash	978-1-910499-30-6 TH Bangladeshi Politicians By Mayar Akash	978-1-910499-10-8 Vigil Subotaged By Mayar Akash	978-1-910499-67-2 F. Ahmed and History By Mukid Choudhury

All books are available on-line, Google the titles and they will take you to the sites where you can acquire copies.
https://www.lulu.com/spotlight/mayarakash3bb00494 [10.11.21]

ISBN/Titles /Image/Author	ISBN/Titles /Image/Author	ISBN/Titles /Image/Author	ISBN/Titles /Image/Author
978-1-910499-43-6 My Life Book 1 By Mayar Akash	978-1-910499-44-3 My Life Book 2 By Mayar Akash	978-1-910499-45-0 My Life Book 3 By Mayar Akash	978-1-910499-46-7 My Life Book 4 By Mayar Akash
978-1-910499-47-4 My Life Book 5 By Mayar Akash	978-1-910499-75-7 Bangladeshis in Manchester - Oral History, Part 1 By M.A. Mustak	978-1-910499-74-0 Peter Fox Artist By Peter Fox	

All books are available on-line, Google the titles and they will take you to the sites where you can acquire copies.

You will also find the on-line catalogue on the following link.
https://www.lulu.com/spotlight/mayarakash3bb00494 [10.11.21]